SpringerBriefs in Well-Being and Quality of Life Research

W0043462

SpringerBriefs in Well-Being and Quality-of-Life Research are concise summaries of cutting-edge research and practical applications across the field of well-being and quality of life research. These compact refereed monographs are under the editorial supervision of an international Advisory Board*. Volumes are 50 to 125 pages (approximately 20,000–70,000 words), with a clear focus. The series covers a range of content from professional to academic such as: snapshots of hot and/or emerging topics, in-depth case studies, and timely reports of state-of-the art analytical techniques. The scope of the series spans the entire field of Well-Being Research and Quality-of-Life Studies, with a view to significantly advance research. The character of the series is international and interdisciplinary and will include research areas such as: health, cross-cultural studies, gender, children, education, work and organizational issues, relationships, job satisfaction, religion, spirituality, ageing from the perspectives of sociology, psychology, philosophy, public health and economics in relation to Well-being and Quality-of-Life research. Volumes in the series may analyze past, present and/or future trends, as well as their determinants and consequences. Both solicited and unsolicited manuscripts are considered for publication in this series. SpringerBriefs in Well-Being and Quality-of-Life Research will be of interest to a wide range of individuals with interest in quality of life studies, including sociologists, psychologists, economists, philosophers, health researchers, as well as practitioners across the social sciences. Briefs will be published as part of Springer's eBook collection, with millions of users worldwide. In addition, Briefs will be available for individual print and electronic purchase. Briefs are characterized by fast, global electronic dissemination, standard publishing contracts, easy-to-use manuscript preparation and formatting guidelines, and expedited production schedules. We aim for publication 8–12 weeks after acceptance.

More information about this series at http://www.springer.com/series/10150

Matthew Bennett • Emma Goodall

Sexual Behaviours and Relationships of Autistics

A Scoping Review

 Springer

Matthew Bennett
Independent Researcher
Adelaide, SA, Australia

Emma Goodall
Healthy Possibilities
Adelaide, SA, Australia

ISSN 2211-7644   ISSN 2211-7652   (electronic)
SpringerBriefs in Well-Being and Quality of Life Research
ISBN 978-3-030-65598-3   ISBN 978-3-030-65599-0   (eBook)
https://doi.org/10.1007/978-3-030-65599-0

This Springer imprint is published by the registered company Springer Nature Switzerland AG.
The registered company address is: Gewerbestrasse 11, 6330 Cham, Switzerland

About This Book

While more research is being published about adults on the autism spectrum, there is still a scarcity of research about their sexual experiences and insights. This SpringerBrief provides a snapshot of the state of research about this topic. Possible articles of interested were located on SpringerLink, PubMed, SAGE, and Taylor and Francis. In total, 23 articles met the pre-determined eligibility criteria; that being published after 1 January 2009 but before 31 December 2019, in English, and sampling autistics. An examination of the bibliographical and relevant citations in the initial 23 articles resulted in the identification and inclusion of an additional four articles.

An analysis of the 27 articles revealed that there is a small amount of research about autistics and their sexual orientation, gender identity and expression, sexual relationships, online sexual activities, and sexual behaviours. A more detailed analysis of this research showed that autistics are more inclined to identify as not being heterosexual or cisgender than allistics (non-autistics). The literature also showed that autistics often tend to obtain information about sexually transmitted infections, appropriate sexual behaviours, and contraception from non-social sources (e.g., the internet), while their allistic peers obtained similar information from their teachers, parents, and other social sources. Despite these findings, the analysis showed that there continues to be many under-researched areas; for example, the coming out and life experiences of LGBTQIA+ autistics, the pregnancy and child-birth experiences of autistic women, and the parenting experiences of autistic parents. This SpringerBrief furnishes the reader with two benefits: First, it provides a concise summary of the current literature about autistics and their sexuality and intimate relationships. Second, it has several recommendations for where more research about this topic can be conducted in the future.

Contents

Chapter 1
Introduction

1.1 A Brief History About the Discovery of Autism Spectrum Conditions

Bleuler (1911) published the earliest known writings about the concept of autism. Although he was the first to mention autism, three decades would pass before Leo Kanner published the first comprehensive description of the condition. In 1943, Leo Kanner (13 June 1894–3 April 1981), an Austrian-American psychiatrist, published our first comprehensive description of autism, a condition that he called *'infantile autism'*. In his 1943 article, called *'Autistic disturbances of affective contact'*, he described the background of eleven children and the three common characteristics of autism that they exhibited; instances of repetitive behaviours, social withdrawal, and restricted language communication skills. In 1981, Lorna Wing would refer to these three characteristics as the *'triad of impairments'* (Wing, 1981). However, research has disputed the view that everyone in the autistic community shares these three characteristics (Van Wijngaarden-Cremers et al., 2014).

In 1944 Hans Asperger (18 February 1906–21 October 1980), an Austrian-born pediatrician, published his German-language clinical observations of four children who exhibited a condition that he called *'Autistic psychopathy'*. He used the term *'psychopathy'* because the children he observed seemed to demonstrate an indifference towards the emotional states of others. When Asperger published his observations, he was not aware of Kanner's writings and vice versa. It is possible that he lacked this awareness because Kanner published his work in English and that communication between the United States of America and Germany was limited due to the Second World War. As Kanner and Asperger progressed through their careers they frequently used the terms *'autistic disturbances'*, *'autistic psychopathy'*, and *'autistic behaviours'*. However, Uta Frith's English translation of Asperger's writings, which occurred in 1991, would clarify these terms. In her translation, Frith replaced the term *'Autistic psychopathy'* with the eponym *'Asperger syndrome'*

© The Author(s), under exclusive license to Springer Nature Switzerland AG 2021
M. Bennett, E. Goodall, *Sexual Behaviours and Relationships of Autistics*,
SpringerBriefs in Well-Being and Quality of Life Research,
https://doi.org/10.1007/978-3-030-65599-0_1

since it removed any pejorative connotations associated with the word *'psychopa-thy'*. Frith also used the word *'autism'* as well in this publication (Frith, 1991a, 1991b).

In 2000, the American Psychiatric Association (APA) published the *Diagnostic and Statistical Manual of Mental Disorders, Fourth Edition - Text Revision* (DSM-IV-TR). In this edition, autism and Asperger syndrome were listed as two distinct conditions which formed two ends of a *'spectrum'* disorder; with Asperger syndrome being at the *'high functioning'* end of the autism spectrum and autism occupying the *'lower functioning'* end of this spectrum. The notion that Asperger syndrome and classic or Kanner's autism occupied two separate ends of an *'autism spectrum'* was expressed by Frankl in 1933 (Frankl, 1933, 1957).

From 1994 until 2013, Wing's notion of a *'triad of impairments'* formed the basis of most diagnostic instruments that were used to diagnose individuals with autism spectrum disorder (Vahia, 2013). However, in May 2013 the APA published the *Diagnostic and Statistical Manual of Mental Disorders, Fifth Edition (DSM-5)*; the successor to the DSM-IV-TR. In the DSM-5, the condition *'Autism Spectrum Disorder'* (ASD) replaced Asperger syndrome and autism. Additionally, in the DSM-5 three severity levels of impairment (i.e., Level 1 Requiring support, Level 2 Requiring substantial support, and Level 3 Requiring very substantial support) were applied to two domains of impairment; *'Social communication'* and *'Restricted, repetitive behaviours'*, rather than the previous triad of impairments. On a sidenote, Murray, Lesser, and Lawson (2005) initially wrote about *'monotropic or single focussed interest'* which is now one of the criteria in the DSM-5 (American Psychiatric Association (APA), 2013). Furthermore, throughout the history of autism *'rigid interests'* and single focused attention have consistently been documented (Lawson, 2009, 2013). Under the DSM-5 a person, for example, could have a Level 1 Social communication and Level 2 Restricted, repetitive behaviours diagnosis while another could have a Level 3 Restricted, repetitive behaviours and Level 2 Social communication diagnosis (APA, 2013).

The prevalence and incidence of ASD has been measured around the world (Elsabbagh et al., 2012). The literature has shown that its prevalence and incidence can change depending on the diagnostic criteria (Bennett & Goodall, 2016a; Gibbs et al., 2012; Maenner et al., 2014) and changes to diagnostic practices (Bennett, Webster, Goodall, & Rowland, 2018a; Hansen et al., 2015; Nassar et al., 2009; Parner et al., 2011). One of the most recent, and arguably reputable, ASD prevalence rates was published by the United States Government's Centre for Disease Control and Prevention (CDC). The CDC operates the Autism and Developmental Disabilities Monitoring (ADDM) network. This network collects data about the number of children who are 8-years-age who have a diagnosis of ASD (Özerk, 2016; Sheldrick & Carter, 2018). The ADDM network revealed that in 2000 and 2002, 1 in 150 children aged 8 years living in the United States of America had an ASD diagnosis. This prevalence rate has risen progressively in the subsequent years, with 1 in 125 children aged 8 years being diagnosed with an ASD in 2004, 1 in 110 in 2006, 1 in 88 in 2008, 1 in 68 in 2010 and 2012, and 1 in 59 in 2014 (Centers for Disease Control and Prevention (CDC), 2018).

1.2   Autistics and Their Sexual Behaviours, Interests, and Insights

In comparison to other fields of autism research, there are relatively few studies about autistics describing their recollections of and views about sexual behaviours, relationships, sexuality, and gender identity. The lack of research about these topics can be attributed to three factors; the historically common act of infantilizing autistic adults, the relatively unorthodox sexual expressions of autistics, and the tendency for researchers to study autistic children instead of autistic adults.

The infantilizing of adult autistics has been proposed as a reason for why not much research has been conducted into their sexual behaviours, insights, and experiences. Bennett et al. (2018a) proposed that the infantilizing of autistics by their parents and society have contributed to the belief that they are immature and not interested in being romantically or sexually involved with others. This is despite research showing that autistics have similar biological timing regarding puberty (May, Pang, O'Connell, & Williams, 2017) and have themselves expressed an interest in having sexual relationships (Bennett, Webster, Goodall, & Rowland, 2018b).

Jang et al. (2014) claimed that most studies on aspects of the autism spectrum have based their conclusions on samples of autistic children. Consequently, there is much less research about autistic adults in adult-specific situations, such as employment settings (Bennett, Webster, Goodall, & Rowland, 2018c). Furthermore, there is also a lack of research about what life is like for autistic senior citizens (Bennett, 2015, 2016; Bennett & Goodall, 2017; Michael, 2016). The limited research about autistic adults has resulted in a lack of appropriate support programs that can help them become fully participating members of society. This lack of research has contributed to suboptimal employment (Roux et al., 2013) and poorer health (Croen et al., 2015; Fortuna et al., 2016) outcomes for autistic adults. The sexual behaviours and interests of autistic adults has also been a topic that has also been largely neglected. One consequence of this lack of research is that we do not have strategies to support LGBTQIA+ autistics (Bennett & Goodall, 2016b).

Several literature reviews have summarised the academic research about autistics and their sexual experiences and insights. However, these studies have typically examined just one specific aspect of this field. For example, van der Miesen, Hurley, and De Vries (2016) and Øien, Cicchetti, and Nordahl-Hansen (2018) examined studies about autistics and gender dysphoria, while Schöttle, Briken, Tüscher, and Turner (2017) explored the research about hypersexual and paraphilic behaviour of *high-functioning autistic women and autistic men*. Unlike previous literature reviews, this scoping review uses a broad focus to help uncover aspects of autistics and their sexual behaviours and interests that have not already been summarised.

References

American Psychiatric Association (APA). (2013). *Diagnostic and statistical manual of mental disorders (DSM-5®)*. American Psychiatric Pub.

Bennett, M. (2015). 'What is it like for adults with ASDs in old age?' A letter about the scant amount of literature on the elderly with autism spectrum disorders. *Age and Ageing, 44*(eLetters Supplement). https://doi.org/10.1093/ageing/el_833

Bennett, M. (2016). "What is life like in the twilight years?" A letter about the scant amount of literature on the elderly with autism spectrum disorders. *Journal of Autism and Developmental Disorders, 46*(5), 1883–1884. https://doi.org/10.1007/s10803-016-2710-z

Bennett, M., & Goodall, E. (2016a). A meta-analysis of DSM-5 autism diagnoses in relation to DSM-IV and DSM-IV-TR. *Review Journal of Autism and Developmental Disorders, 3*(2), 119–124. https://doi.org/10.1007/s40489-016-0070-4

Bennett, M., & Goodall, E. (2016b). Towards an agenda for research for lesbian, gay, bisexual, transgendered and/or intersexed people with an autism spectrum diagnosis. *Journal of Autism and Developmental Disorders, 46*(9), 3190–3192. https://doi.org/10.1007/s10803-016-2844-z

Bennett, M., & Goodall, E. (2017). Elderly with autism spectrum disorders. In F. Volkmar (Ed.), *Encyclopaedia of autism spectrum disorders*. New York, NY: Springer. https://doi.org/10.1007/978-1-4614-6435-8_102195-1

Bennett, M., Webster, A. A., Goodall, E., & Rowland, S. (2018a). Exploring the identity of autistic individuals: Reconstructing the autism epidemic myth. In *Life on the autism spectrum* (pp. 17–35). Singapore: Springer. https://doi.org/10.1007/978-981-13-3359-0_2

Bennett, M., Webster, A. A., Goodall, E., & Rowland, S. (2018b). Intimacy and romance across the autism spectrum: Unpacking the "not interested in sex" myth. In *Life on the autism spectrum* (pp. 195–211). Singapore: Springer. https://doi.org/10.1007/978-981-13-3359-0_10

Bennett, M., Webster, A. A., Goodall, E., & Rowland, S. (2018c). Supporting self-efficacy and self-determination on the autism spectrum: Refuting the "autism can be outgrown" myth. In *Life on the autism spectrum* (pp. 213–232). Singapore: Springer. https://doi.org/10.1007/978-981-13-3359-0_11

Bleuler, E. (1911). Dementia Praecox oder Gruppe der Schizophrenien. In G. Aschaffenburg (Ed.), *Handbuch der Psychiatrie. Leipzig* (pp. 1–420). Vienna: Deuticke.

Centers for Disease Control and Prevention. (2018). *Data & statistics*. Retrieved from https://www.cdc.gov/ncbddd/autism/data.html

Croen, L. A., Zerbo, O., Qian, Y., Massolo, M. L., Rich, S., Sidney, S., et al. (2015). The health status of adults on the autism spectrum. *Autism, 19*(7), 814–823. https://doi.org/10.1177/1362361315577517

Dunn, D. S., & Andrews, E. E. (2015). Person-first and identity-first language: Developing psychologists' cultural competence using disability language. *American Psychologist, 70*(3), 255.

Elsabbagh, M., Divan, G., Koh, Y. J., Kim, Y. S., Kauchali, S., Marcín, C., et al. (2012). Global prevalence of autism and other pervasive developmental disorders. *Autism Research, 5*(3), 160–179. https://doi.org/10.1002/aur.239

Fortuna, R. J., Robinson, L., Smith, T. H., Meccarello, J., Bullen, B., Nobis, K., et al. (2016). Health conditions and functional status in adults with autism: A cross-sectional evaluation. *Journal of General Internal Medicine, 31*(1), 77–84. https://doi.org/10.1007/s11606-015-3509-x

Frankl, G. (1933). Ordering and obeying. *Zeitschrift fur Kinderforschung, 42*, 464.

Frankl, G. (1957). *Autism in childhood: An attempt of an analysis (unpublished manuscript)*. Lawrence, KS: Kenneth Spencer Research Library, The University of Kansas.

Frith, U. (1991a). Asperger and his syndrome. *Autism and Asperger Syndrome, 14*, 1–36.

Frith, U. (1991b). *Autism and Asperger Syndrome*. Cambridge: Cambridge University Press.

Gibbs, V., Aldridge, F., Chandler, F., Witzlsperger, E., & Smith, K. (2012). Brief report: an exploratory study comparing diagnostic outcomes for autism spectrum disorders under DSM-

IV-TR with the proposed DSM-5 revision. *Journal of Autism and Developmental Disorders, 42* (8), 1750–1756. https://doi.org/10.1007/s10803-012-1560-6

Hansen, S. N., Schendel, D. E., & Parner, E. T. (2015). Explaining the increase in the prevalence of autism spectrum disorders: The proportion attributable to changes in reporting practices. *JAMA Pediatrics, 169*(1), 56–62. https://doi.org/10.1001/jamapediatrics.2014.1893

Jang, J., Matson, J. L., Adams, H. L., Konst, M. J., Cervantes, P. E., & Goldin, R. L. (2014). What are the ages of persons studied in autism research: A 20-year review. *Research in Autism Spectrum Disorders, 8*(12), 1756–1760. https://doi.org/10.1016/j.rasd.2014.08.008

Kenny, L., Hattersley, C., Molins, B., Buckley, C., Povey, C., & Pellicano, E. (2016). Which terms should be used to describe autism? Perspectives from the UK autism community. *Autism, 20*(4), 442–462. https://doi.org/10.1177/1362361315588200

Lawson, W. (2009). *Single Attention and associated Cognition in autism (SACCA).* Unpublished thesis, Deakin University, Australia.

Lawson, W. (2013). Autism spectrum conditions: The pathophysiological basis for inattention and the new Diagnostic and Statistical Manual of Mental Disorders (DSM-V). *OA Autism, 1*(1), 1.

Maenner, M. J., Rice, C. E., Arneson, C. L., Cunniff, C., Schieve, L. A., Carpenter, L. A., et al. (2014). Potential impact of DSM-5 criteria on autism spectrum disorder prevalence estimates. *JAMA Psychiatry, 71*(3), 292–300. https://doi.org/10.1001/jamapsychiatry.2013.3893

May, T., Pang, K. C., O'Connell, M. A., & Williams, K. (2017). Typical pubertal timing in an Australian population of girls and boys with autism spectrum disorder. *Journal of Autism and Developmental Disorders, 47*(12), 3983–3993. https://doi.org/10.1007/s10803-017-3281-3

Michael, C. (2016). Why we need research about autism and ageing. *Autism, 20*(5), 515–516. https://doi.org/10.1177/1362361316647224

Murray, D., Lesser, M., & Lawson, W. (2005). Attention, monotropism and the diagnostic criteria for autism. *Autism, 9*(2), 139–156. https://doi.org/10.1177/1362361305051398

Nassar, N., Dixon, G., Bourke, J., Bower, C., Glasson, E., De Klerk, N., et al. (2009). Autism spectrum disorders in young children: Effect of changes in diagnostic practices. *International Journal of Epidemiology, 38*(5), 1245–1254. https://doi.org/10.1093/ije/dyp260

Øien, R. A., Cicchetti, D. V., & Nordahl-Hansen, A. (2018). Gender dysphoria, sexuality and autism spectrum disorders: A systematic map review. *Journal of Autism and Developmental Disorders, 48*(12), 4028–4037. https://doi.org/10.1007/s10803-018-3686-7

Özerk, K. (2016). The issue of prevalence of autism/ASD. *International Electronic Journal of Elementary Education, 9*(2), 263–306.

Parner, E., Thorsen, P., Dixon, G., Klerk, N., Leonard, H., Nassar, N., et al. (2011). A comparison of autism prevalence trends in Denmark and Western Australia. *Journal of Autism and Developmental Disorders, 41*(12), 1601–1608. https://doi.org/10.1007/s10803-011-1186-0

Roux, A. M., Shattuck, P. T., Cooper, B. P., Anderson, K. A., Wagner, M., & Narendorf, S. C. (2013). Postsecondary employment experiences among young adults with an autism spectrum disorder. *Journal of the American Academy of Child and Adolescent Psychiatry, 52*(9), 931–939. https://doi.org/10.1016/j.jaac.2013.05.019

Schöttle, D., Briken, P., Tüscher, O., & Turner, D. (2017). Sexuality in autism: Hypersexual and paraphilic behavior in women and men with high-functioning autism spectrum disorder. *Dialogues in Clinical Neuroscience, 19*(4), 381–393.

Sheldrick, R. C., & Carter, A. S. (2018). State-level trends in the prevalence of Autism Spectrum Disorder (ASD) from 2000 to 2012: A reanalysis of findings from the autism and developmental disabilities network. *Journal of Autism and Developmental Disorders, 48*(9), 3086–3092. https://doi.org/10.1007/s10803-018-3568-z

Vahia, V. N. (2013). Diagnostic and statistical manual of mental disorders 5: A quick glance. *Indian Journal of Psychiatry, 55*(3), 220–223. https://doi.org/10.4103/0019-5545.117131

van der Miesen, A. I., Hurley, H., & De Vries, A. L. (2016). Gender dysphoria and autism spectrum disorder: A narrative review. *International Review of Psychiatry, 28*(1), 70–80. https://doi.org/10.3109/09540261.2015.1111199

Van Wijngaarden-Cremers, P. J., van Eeten, E., Groen, W. B., Van Deurzen, P. A., Oosterling, I. J., & Van der Gaag, R. J. (2014). Gender and age differences in the core triad of impairments in autism spectrum disorders: A systematic review and meta-analysis. *Journal of Autism and Developmental Disorders, 44*(3), 627–635. https://doi.org/10.1007/s10803-013-1913-9

Wing, L. (1981). Language, social, and cognitive impairments in autism and severe mental retardation. *Journal of Autism and Developmental Disorders, 11*(1), 31–44. https://doi.org/10.1007/BF01531339

Chapter 2
Methodology

2.1 Scoping Review Procedure

The methodological procedures that were used to conduct this scoping review was based on Arksey and O'Malley's (2005) five-stage framework for conducting a scoping review. These five-stages are:

1. Formulating the initial research question
2. Identifying relevant studies
3. Select relevant studies
4. Charting the data, and
5. Collecting, summarising, and reporting the results.

Step One—Formulating the Initial Research Question
The first step in conducting any scoping study is to formulate a set of research questions. Generally, research questions should be broad and clear so that they can give the researcher the opportunity to collect and analyse an extensive range of research (Arksey & O'Malley, 2005). However, Levac, Colquhoun, and O'Brien (2010) cautions that sometimes research questions that are too broad often lack enough specificity, which can undermine the subsequent stages of the research process, such as identifying relevant studies and deciding what studies to include or exclude. To avoid this outcome, Levac et al. suggests that researchers use a general research question in combination with a clear purpose for conducting the scoping study. As Levac et al. (2010, p. 5) explains:

> Linking a clear purpose for undertaking a scoping study to a well-defined research question at the first stage of the framework will help to provide a clear rationale for completing the study and facilitating decision making about study selection and data extraction later in the methodological process.

The focus of this scoping review was to explore and summarise the key findings in the peer-reviewed literature about autistics and their sexual behaviours and

M. Bennett, E. Goodall, *Sexual Behaviours and Relationships of Autistics*,
SpringerBriefs in Well-Being and Quality of Life Research,
https://doi.org/10.1007/978-3-030-65599-0_2

relationship experiences. To fulfil this objective four research questions were formulated to guide the search and to ensure that a substantial range of literature was captured about these topics.

1. What sexual behaviours were explored in the collected literature?
2. What are the relationship experiences of adolescents and adults on the autism spectrum?
3. What are the birthing and parenting experiences of women on the autism spectrum?
4. What are the domestic/family violence experiences of adolescents and adults on the autism spectrum?

Step Two—Identifying Relevant Studies

To identify a broad range of studies, Arksey and O'Malley (2005) suggest that key words that are general to the topic should be used instead of key words that are specific. For example, instead of using the term *'heterosexual'* and *'homosexual'*, which were deemed to be too specific, the general term *'sexuality'* was used instead. In the context of this scoping review the search terms entered were *'ASD'* OR *'autis*'* AND *'Sex*'* OR *'Relation*'*. This permutation of phrases was entered into four databases; SpringerLink, PubMed, Taylor and Francis, and SAGE.

Step Three—Selecting Relevant Studies

The third step outlined by Arksey and O'Malley (2005) involves selecting from the search results studies that appear likely to answer the research questions and ultimately address the focus of the scoping review. For this scoping review, as outlined below, this step involved two phases.

The first phase involved entering the search terms into the search field of the database. The titles of the articles were then examined and if the article was deemed to be of interest then its abstract was analysed. If it was believed that the abstract contained information that could help answer the research questions, along with the focus of the scoping study, then the article was examined relative to the eligibility criteria (see Table 2.1). After duplicates were removed, 61 articles were deemed to be of interest. However, 38 did not meet the eligibility criteria (see Table 2.2), resulting in 23 studies that met the eligibility criteria and worthy of examination (Barnett, 2017; Barnett & Maticka-Tyndale, 2015; Brown-Lavoie, Viecili, & Weiss, 2014; Bush, 2019; Byers & Nichols, 2014; Byers, Nichols, & Voyer, 2013; Byers, Nichols, Voyer, & Reilly, 2013; Cheak-Zamora, Teti, Maurer-Batjer, O'Connor, & Randolph, 2019; Cooper, Smith, & Russell, 2018; De Vries, Noens, Cohen-Kettenis, van Berckelaer-Onnes, & Doreleijers, 2010; Dewinter, De Graaf, & Begeer, 2017; Dewinter, Van Parys, Vermeiren, & Van Nieuwenhuizen, 2017; Dewinter, Vermeiren, Vanwesenbeeck, Lobbestael, & van Nieuwenhuizen, 2015; Dewinter, Vermeiren, Vanwesenbeeck, & Van Nieuwenhuizen, 2016a; Hancock, Stokes, & Mesibov, 2019; Hannah & Stagg, 2016; May, Pang, & Williams, 2017; Mogavero & Hsu, 2019; Pearlman-Avnion, Cohen, & Eldan, 2017; Roth & Gillis, 2015; Strang et al., 2018; Strunz et al., 2017; van der Miesen, Hurley, Bal, & de Vries, 2018).

Table 2.1 Inclusion and exclusion criteria

Criterion	Inclusion	Exclusion	Justification
Time period	Studies published after 1 January 2009 and before 31 December 2019	Studies published before 1 January 2009 or after 31 December 2019	This scoping review was only concerned with publications from the last decade. The databases were searched in January 2020. This date range was selected to obtain the most contemporary literature as possible.
Language	Studies published in English	Studies published in languages other than English	This scoping review was only concerned with examining research published in English since it was the researchers' native language.
Type of article	Studies that included samples of autistic adults, autistic adolescents, and/or autistic children	Studies that did not contain a sample of autistic participants (i.e., letters to the editor, literature reviews, and case studies)	The researchers were only interested in exploring the experiences of autistics not those of other stakeholders.

Table 2.2 Studies retrieved and excluded during phase one

Reason	Studies not eligible
Publications that were not articles	
Letter to the editor	Bennett and Goodall (2016)
Literature reviews or meta-analysis studies	Beddows and Brooks (2016), Hancock, Stokes, and Mesibov (2017), Øien, Cicchetti, and Nordahl-Hansen (2018), Pecora, Mesibov, and Stokes (2016), Sala, Hooley, Attwood, Mesibov, and Stokes (2019), Schöttle, Briken, Tüscher, and Turner (2017), Sevlever, Roth, and Gillis (2013) and van der Miesen, Hurley, and De Vries (2016)
Academic opinion pieces	Ballan and Freyer (2017), Curtiss and Ebata (2016), Kellaher (2015) and Parchomiuk (2019)
Book reviews	Drahota (2010) and Glasberg (2010)
Case studies	Lemaire, Thomazeau, and Bonnet-Brilhault (2014) and Violeta and Langer (2017)
Retrospective chart reviews	Rudolph, Lundin, Åhs, Dalman, and Kosidou (2018)
Studies that do not involve autistic insights and experiences (e.g., A study might investigate autism symptomology in juvenile suspects of sex offences; Autistic features in children and adolescents with gender dysphoria; Samples of paediatricians who regularly care for autistic youth)	Dekker et al. (2015), Pasterski, Gilligan, and Curtis (2014) and Qualls, Hartmann, and Paulson (2018)

(continued)

Table 2.2 (continued)

Reason	Studies not eligible
Publications that involved parents or care-givers of autistics, but not autistics themselves	Ballan (2012), Corona, Fox, Christodulu, and Worlock (2016), Dekker et al. (2015), Dewinter, Vermeiren, Vanwesenbeeck, and Van Nieuwenhuizen (2016b), Fernandes et al. (2016), Hartmann et al. (2019), Hellemans, Roeyers, Leplae, Dewaele, and Deboutte (2010), Holmes and Himle (2014), Holmes, Strassberg, and Himle (2019), Mackin, Loew, Gonzalez, Tykol, and Christensen (2016), May, Pang, O'Connell, and Williams (2017), Nichols and Blakeley-Smith (2009) and Pryde and Jahoda (2018)

The second phase involved searching the reference lists of the 23 studies which met the eligibility criteria for phase one. The purpose of this search was to find additional articles that were not identified from the search procedures used in the first phase. Based on this search procedure, 57 articles were identified to be of interest. However, after applying the same eligibility criteria used in phase one, 53 did not meet the eligibility criteria (see Table 2.3), resulting in only four studies that met the eligibility criteria and worthy of examination (George & Stokes, 2018; Gilmour, Schalomon, & Smith, 2012; Kanfiszer, Davies, & Collins, 2017; Mehzabin & Stokes, 2011).

Table 2.3 Studies excluded during phase two

Reason	Studies not eligible
Publications which were not articles	
Literature reviews or meta-analysis studies	Dewinter, Vermeiren, Vanwesenbeeck, and van Nieuwenhuizen (2013), Glidden, Bouman, Jones, and Arcelus (2016), Gougeon (2010), van Schalkwyk, Klingensmith, and Volkmar (2015)
Academic opinion pieces	Chan and John (2012), Hatton and Tector (2010), Holmes et al. (2014), Travers and Tincani (2010), Tullis and Zangrillo (2013) and Wolfe, Condo, and Hardaway (2009)
Case studies	Bejerot and Eriksson (2014), Chan and Saluja (2011), Griffin-Shelley (2010), Jacobs, Rachlin, Erickson-Schroth, and Janssen (2014) and Perera, Gadambanathan, and Weerasiri (2011)
Retrospective chart reviews	Janssen, Huang, and Duncan (2016), Shumer, Reisner, Edwards-Leeper, and Tishelman (2016) and Strang et al. (2014)
Studies that do not involve autistic insights and experiences (e.g., A study might investigate autism symptomology in juvenile suspects of	't Hart-Kerkhoffs et al. (2009), Jones et al. (2012), Kalyva (2010), Skagerberg, Di Ceglie,

(continued)

Table 2.3 (continued)

Reason	Studies not eligible
sex offences; Autistic features in children and adolescents with gender dysphoria; Samples of paediatricians who have cared for autistic youth)	and Carmichael (2015) and VanderLaan, Leef, Wood, Hughes, and Zucker (2015)
Publication involves parents or caregivers of autistics, but not autistics themselves	Holmes, Himle, and Strassberg (2016) and Visser et al. (2015)
Study was published outside the date range (i.e., before 1 January 2009 or after 31 December 2019)	Byers et al. (2003), Engström, Ekström, and Emilsson (2003), Gallucci, Hackerman, and Schmidt (2005), Hearn, O'Sullivan, and Dudley (2003), Hellemans, Colson, Verbraeken, Vermeiren, and Deboutte (2007), Kohn, Fahum, Ratzoni, and Apter (1998), Koller (2000), Konstantareas and Lunsky (1997), Kraemer, Delsignore, Gundelfinger, Schnyder, and Hepp (2005), Landén and Rasmussen (1997), Lunsky and Konstantareas (1998), Meister, Norlock, Honeyman, and Pierce (1994), Milton, Duggan, Latham, Egan, and Tantam (2002), Mukaddes (2002), Orsmond, Krauss, and Seltzer (2004), Ousley and Mesibov (1991), Ray, Marks, and Bray-Garretson (2004), Realmuto and Ruble (1999), Renty and Roeyers (2007), Ruble and Dalrymple (1993), Stokes and Kaur (2005), Stokes, Newton, and Kaur (2007), Sullivan and Caterino (2008), Tarnai and Wolfe (2008), Tateno, Tateno, and Saito (2008), Torisky (1985), van Bourgondien, Reichle, and Palmer (1997) and Williams, Allard, and Sears (1996)

Step Four—Charting the Data
The fourth stage of Arksey and O'Malley's (2005) scoping review framework involves identifying and collating the key features in the collected articles. The key features that were identified, included:

1. Sample characteristics (e.g., age range of the sample, number of participants in the sample, gender composition of the sample), and
2. Key themes of the studies (e.g., relationship experiences).

The purpose of mapping these key features was to provide a comprehensive and holistic overview of the state of the research about autism and sexual behaviours and relationships.

Step Five—Collecting, Summarising, and Reporting the Results
The fifth and final step in Arksey and O'Malley's (2005) scoping review framework involves summarising the key features of the study and reporting the findings. To complete this step the authors read the contents of the studies that were identified from phases one and two. When a theme embedded in the article was identified, a key word was allocated to summarise the theme. The key words were then listed and

refined until a succinct list of key themes were formulated. This list helped guide the reporting of the main results.

2.2   Conclusion

This chapter has provided a clear and concise explanation about the processes used to collect and examine relevant studies. This scoping review is based on Arksey and O'Malley's (2005) five-stage framework for conducting a scoping review. This chapter showed that 29 studies were identified that met the eligibility criterion. In the next chapter an aggregate summary of these results and the main themes discovered in this body of research are explained.

References

't Hart-Kerkhoffs, L. A., Jansen, L. M., Doreleijers, T. A., Vermeiren, R., Minderaa, R. B., & Hartman, C. A. (2009). Autism spectrum disorder symptoms in juvenile suspects of sex offenses. *The Journal of Clinical Psychiatry, 70*(2), 266–272.

Arksey, H., & O'Malley, L. (2005). Scoping studies: Towards a methodological framework. *International Journal of Social Research Methodology, 8*(1), 19–32. https://doi.org/10.1080/1364557032000119616

Ballan, M. S. (2012). Parental perspectives of communication about sexuality in families of children with autism spectrum disorders. *Journal of Autism and Developmental Disorders, 42*(5), 676–684. https://doi.org/10.1007/s10803-011-1293-y

Ballan, M. S., & Freyer, M. B. (2017). Autism spectrum disorder, adolescence, and sexuality education: Suggested interventions for mental health professionals. *Sexuality and Disability, 35*(2), 261–273. https://doi.org/10.1007/s11195-017-9477-9

Barnett, J. P. (2017). Intersectional harassment and deviant embodiment among Autistic adults:(dis) ability, gender and sexuality. *Culture, Health & Sexuality, 19*(11), 1210–1224. https://doi.org/10.1080/13691058.2017.1309070

Barnett, J. P., & Maticka-Tyndale, E. (2015). Qualitative exploration of sexual experiences among adults on the autism spectrum: Implications for sex education. *Perspectives on Sexual and Reproductive Health, 47*(4), 171–179. https://doi.org/10.1363/47e5715

Beddows, N., & Brooks, R. (2016). Inappropriate sexual behaviour in adolescents with autism spectrum disorder: What education is recommended and why. *Early Intervention in Psychiatry, 10*(4), 282–289. https://doi.org/10.1111/eip.12265

Bejerot, S., & Eriksson, J. M. (2014). Sexuality and gender role in autism spectrum disorder: A case control study. *PLoS One, 9*(1), e87961. https://doi.org/10.1371/journal.pone.0087961

Bennett, M., & Goodall, E. (2016). Towards an agenda for research for lesbian, gay, bisexual, transgendered and/or intersexed people with an Autism Spectrum Diagnosis. *Journal of Autism and Developmental Disorders, 46*(9), 3190–3192. https://doi.org/10.1007/s10803-016-2844-z

Brown-Lavoie, S. M., Viecili, M. A., & Weiss, J. A. (2014). Sexual knowledge and victimization in adults with autism spectrum disorders. *Journal of Autism and Developmental Disorders, 44*(9), 2185–2196. https://doi.org/10.1007/s10803-014-2093-y

Bush, H. H. (2019). Dimensions of sexuality among young women, with and without autism, with predominantly sexual minority identities. *Sexuality and Disability, 37*(2), 275–292. https://doi.org/10.1007/s11195-018-9532-1

Byers, E. S., & Nichols, S. (2014). Sexual satisfaction of high-functioning adults with autism spectrum disorder. *Sexuality and Disability, 32*(3), 365–382. https://doi.org/10.1007/s11195-014-9351-y

Byers, E. S., Nichols, S., & Voyer, S. D. (2013). Challenging stereotypes: Sexual functioning of single adults with high functioning autism spectrum disorder. *Journal of Autism and Developmental Disorders, 43*(11), 2617–2627. https://doi.org/10.1007/s10803-013-1813-z

Byers, E. S., Nichols, S., Voyer, S. D., & Reilly, G. (2013). Sexual well-being of a community sample of high-functioning adults on the autism spectrum who have been in a romantic relationship. *Autism, 17*(4), 418–433. https://doi.org/10.1177/1362361311431950

Byers, E. S., Sears, H. A., Voyer, S. D., Thurlow, J. L., Cohen, J. N., & Weaver, A. D. (2003). An adolescent perspective on sexual health education at school and at home: I. High school students. *Canadian Journal of Human Sexuality, 12*(1), 19–33.

Chan, J., & John, R. M. (2012). Sexuality and sexual health in children and adolescents with autism. *The Journal for Nurse Practitioners, 8*(4), 306–315. https://doi.org/10.1016/j.nurpra.2012.01.020

Chan, L. G., & Saluja, B. (2011). Sexual offending and improvement in autistic characteristics after acquired brain injury: A case report. *Australian and New Zealand Journal of Psychiatry, 45*(10), 902–903. https://doi.org/10.3109/00048674.2011.589371

Cheak-Zamora, N. C., Teti, M., Maurer-Batjer, A., O'Connor, K. V., & Randolph, J. K. (2019). Sexual and relationship interest, knowledge, and experiences among adolescents and young adults with autism spectrum disorder. *Archives of Sexual Behavior, 48*(8), 2605–2615. https://doi.org/10.1007/s10508-019-1445-2

Cooper, K., Smith, L. G., & Russell, A. J. (2018). Gender identity in autism: Sex differences in social affiliation with gender groups. *Journal of Autism and Developmental Disorders, 48*(12), 3995–4006. https://doi.org/10.1007/s10803-018-3590-1

Corona, L. L., Fox, S. A., Christodulu, K. V., & Worlock, J. A. (2016). Providing education on sexuality and relationships to adolescents with autism spectrum disorder and their parents. *Sexuality and Disability, 34*(2), 199–214. https://doi.org/10.1007/s11195-015-9424-6

Curtiss, S. L., & Ebata, A. T. (2016). Building capacity to deliver sex education to individuals with autism. *Sexuality and Disability, 34*(1), 27–47. https://doi.org/10.1007/s11195-016-9429-9

De Vries, A. L., Noens, I. L., Cohen-Kettenis, P. T., van Berckelaer-Onnes, I. A., & Doreleijers, T. A. (2010). Autism spectrum disorders in gender dysphoric children and adolescents. *Journal of Autism and Developmental Disorders, 40*(8), 930–936. https://doi.org/10.1007/s10803-010-0935-9

Dekker, L. P., Hartman, C. A., van der Vegt, E. J., Verhulst, F. C., van Oort, F. V., & Greaves-Lord, K. (2015). The longitudinal relation between childhood autistic traits and psychosexual problems in early adolescence: The Tracking Adolescents' Individual Lives Survey study. *Autism, 19*(6), 684–693. https://doi.org/10.1177/1362361314547114

Dekker, L. P., van der Vegt, E. J., Visser, K., Tick, N., Boudesteijn, F., Verhulst, F. C., et al. (2015). Improving psychosexual knowledge in adolescents with autism spectrum disorder: Pilot of the tackling teenage training program. *Journal of Autism and Developmental Disorders, 45*(6), 1532–1540. https://doi.org/10.1007/s10803-014-2301-9

Dewinter, J., De Graaf, H., & Begeer, S. (2017). Sexual orientation, gender identity, and romantic relationships in adolescents and adults with autism spectrum disorder. *Journal of Autism and Developmental Disorders, 47*(9), 2927–2934. https://doi.org/10.1007/s10803-017-3199-9

Dewinter, J., Van Parys, H., Vermeiren, R., & Van Nieuwenhuizen, C. (2017). Adolescent boys with an autism spectrum disorder and their experience of sexuality: An interpretative phenomenological analysis. *Autism, 21*(1), 75–82. https://doi.org/10.1177/1362361315627134

Dewinter, J., Vermeiren, R., Vanwesenbeeck, I., Lobbestael, J., & van Nieuwenhuizen, C. (2015). Sexuality in adolescent boys with autism spectrum disorder: Self-reported behaviours and attitudes. *Journal of Autism and Developmental Disorders, 45*(3), 731–741. https://doi.org/10.1007/s10803-014-2226-3

Dewinter, J., Vermeiren, R., Vanwesenbeeck, I., & van Nieuwenhuizen, C. (2013). Autism and normative sexual development: A narrative review. *Journal of Clinical Nursing, 22*(23–24), 3467–3483. https://doi.org/10.1111/jocn.12397

Dewinter, J., Vermeiren, R. R. J. M., Vanwesenbeeck, I., & Van Nieuwenhuizen, C. (2016a). Adolescent boys with autism spectrum disorder growing up: Follow-up of self-reported sexual experience. *European Child & Adolescent Psychiatry, 25*(9), 969–978. https://doi.org/10.1007/s00787-016-0816-7

Dewinter, J., Vermeiren, R. R. J. M., Vanwesenbeeck, I., & Van Nieuwenhuizen, C. (2016b). Parental awareness of sexual experience in adolescent boys with autism spectrum disorder. *Journal of Autism and Developmental Disorders, 46*(2), 713–719. https://doi.org/10.1007/s10803-015-2622-3

Drahota, A. (2010). S. Hendrickx: Love, sex & long-term relationships: what people with asperger syndrome really really want. *Journal of Autism and Developmental Disorders, 40*(2), 260–261. https://doi.org/10.1007/s10803-009-0805-5

Engström, I., Ekström, L., & Emilsson, B. (2003). Psychosocial functioning in a group of Swedish adults with Asperger syndrome or high-functioning autism. *Autism, 7*(1), 99–110. https://doi.org/10.1177/1362361303007001008

Fernandes, L. C., Gillberg, C. I., Cederlund, M., Hagberg, B., Gillberg, C., & Billstedt, E. (2016). Aspects of sexuality in adolescents and adults diagnosed with autism spectrum disorders in childhood. *Journal of Autism and Developmental Disorders, 46*(9), 3155–3165. https://doi.org/10.1007/s10803-016-2855-9

Gallucci, G., Hackerman, F., & Schmidt, C. W. (2005). Gender identity disorder in an adult male with Asperger's syndrome. *Sexuality and Disability, 23*(1), 35–40. https://doi.org/10.1007/s11195-004-2078-4

George, R., & Stokes, M. A. (2018). A quantitative analysis of mental health among sexual and gender minority groups in ASD. *Journal of Autism and Developmental Disorders, 48*(6), 2052–2063. https://doi.org/10.1007/s10803-018-3469-1

Gilmour, L., Schalomon, P. M., & Smith, V. (2012). Sexuality in a community based sample of adults with autism spectrum disorder. *Research in Autism Spectrum Disorders, 6*(1), 313–318. https://doi.org/10.1016/j.rasd.2011.06.003

Glasberg, B. (2010). Sarah Attwood: Making sense of sex: A forthright guide to puberty, sex, and relationships for people with Asperger's syndrome. *Journal of Autism and Developmental Disorders, 40*(3), 392–393. https://doi.org/10.1007/s10803-009-0900-7

Glidden, D., Bouman, W. P., Jones, B. A., & Arcelus, J. (2016). Gender dysphoria and autism spectrum disorder: A systematic review of the literature. *Sexual Medicine Reviews, 4*(1), 3–14. https://doi.org/10.1016/j.sxmr.2015.10.003

Gougeon, N. A. (2010). Sexuality and autism: A critical review of selected literature using a social-relational model of disability. *American Journal of Sexuality Education, 5*(4), 328–361. https://doi.org/10.1080/15546128.2010.527237

Griffin-Shelley, E. (2010). An Asperger's adolescent sex addict, sex offender: A case study. *Sexual Addiction & Compulsivity, 17*(1), 46–64. https://doi.org/10.1080/10720161003646450

Hancock, G., Stokes, M. A., & Mesibov, G. (2019). Differences in romantic relationship experiences for individuals with an autism spectrum disorder. *Sexuality and Disability*, 1–15. https://doi.org/10.1007/s11195-019-09573-8

Hancock, G. I., Stokes, M. A., & Mesibov, G. B. (2017). Socio-sexual functioning in autism spectrum disorder: A systematic review and meta-analyses of existing literature. *Autism Research, 10*(11), 1823–1833. https://doi.org/10.1002/aur.1831

Hannah, L. A., & Stagg, S. D. (2016). Experiences of sex education and sexual awareness in young adults with autism spectrum disorder. *Journal of Autism and Developmental Disorders, 46*(12), 3678–3687. https://doi.org/10.1007/s10803-016-2906-2

Hartmann, K., Urbano, M. R., Raffaele, C. T., Qualls, L. R., Williams, T. V., Warren, C., et al. (2019). Sexuality in the Autism Spectrum Study (SASS): Reports from young adults and parents. *Journal of Autism and Developmental Disorders, 49*(9), 3638–3655. https://doi.org/10. 1007/s10803-019-04077-y

Hatton, S., & Tector, A. (2010). FOCUS ON PRACTICE: Sexuality and relationship education for young people with autistic spectrum disorder: Curriculum change and staff support. *British Journal of Special Education, 37*(2), 69–76. https://doi.org/10.1111/j.1467-8578.2010.00466.x

Hearn, K. D., O'Sullivan, L. F., & Dudley, C. D. (2003). Assessing reliability of early adolescent girls' reports of romantic and sexual behavior. *Archives of Sexual Behavior, 32*(6), 513–521. https://doi.org/10.1023/A:1026033426547

Hellemans, H., Colson, K., Verbraeken, C., Vermeiren, R., & Deboutte, D. (2007). Sexual behavior in high-functioning male adolescents and young adults with autism spectrum disorder. *Journal of Autism and Developmental Disorders, 37*(2), 260–269. https://doi.org/10.1007/s10803-006-0159-1

Hellemans, H., Roeyers, H., Leplae, W., Dewaele, T., & Deboutte, D. (2010). Sexual behavior in male adolescents and young adults with autism spectrum disorder and borderline/mild mental retardation. *Sexuality and Disability, 28*(2), 93–104. https://doi.org/10.1007/s11195-009-9145-9

Holmes, L. G., & Himle, M. B. (2014). Brief report: Parent–child sexuality communication and autism spectrum disorders. *Journal of Autism and Developmental Disorders, 44*(11), 2964–2970. https://doi.org/10.1007/s10803-014-2146-2

Holmes, L. G., Himle, M. B., Sewell, K. K., Carbone, P. S., Strassberg, D. S., & Murphy, N. A. (2014). Addressing sexuality in youth with autism spectrum disorders: Current pediatric practices and barriers. *Journal of Developmental & Behavioral Pediatrics, 35*(3), 172–178. https://doi.org/10.1097/DBP.0000000000000030

Holmes, L. G., Himle, M. B., & Strassberg, D. S. (2016). Parental romantic expectations and parent–child sexuality communication in autism spectrum disorders. *Autism, 20*(6), 687–699. https://doi.org/10.1177/1362361315602371

Holmes, L. G., Strassberg, D. S., & Himle, M. B. (2019). Family sexuality communication for adolescent girls on the autism spectrum. *Journal of Autism and Developmental Disorders, 49* (6), 2403–2416. https://doi.org/10.1007/s10803-019-03904-6

Jacobs, L. A., Rachlin, K., Erickson-Schroth, L., & Janssen, A. (2014). Gender dysphoria and co-occurring autism spectrum disorders: Review, case examples, and treatment considerations. *LGBT Health, 1*(4), 277–282. https://doi.org/10.1089/lgbt.2013.0045

Janssen, A., Huang, H., & Duncan, C. (2016). Gender variance among youth with autism spectrum disorders: A retrospective chart review. *Transgender Health, 1*(1), 63–68. https://doi.org/10. 1089/trgh.2015.0007

Jones, R. M., Wheelwright, S., Farrell, K., Martin, E., Green, R., Di Ceglie, D., et al. (2012). Brief report: Female-to-male transsexual people and autistic traits. *Journal of Autism and Developmental Disorders, 42*(2), 301–306. https://doi.org/10.1007/s10803-011-1227-8

Kalyva, E. (2010). Teachers' perspectives of the sexuality of children with autism spectrum disorders. *Research in Autism Spectrum Disorders, 4*(3), 433–437. https://doi.org/10.1016/j. rasd.2009.10.014

Kanfiszer, L., Davies, F., & Collins, S. (2017). 'I was just so different': The experiences of women diagnosed with an autism spectrum disorder in adulthood in relation to gender and social relationships. *Autism, 21*(6), 661–669. https://doi.org/10.1177/1362361316687987

Kellaher, D. C. (2015). Sexual behavior and autism spectrum disorders: An update and discussion. *Current Psychiatry Reports, 17*(4), 25. https://doi.org/10.1007/s11920-015-0562-4

Kohn, Y., Fahum, T., Ratzoni, G., & Apter, A. (1998). Aggression and sexual offense in Asperger's syndrome. *The Israel Journal of Psychiatry and Related Sciences, 35*(4), 293.

Koller, R. (2000). Sexuality and adolescents with autism. *Sexuality and Disability, 18*(2), 125–135. https://doi.org/10.1023/A:1005567030442

Konstantareas, M. M., & Lunsky, Y. J. (1997). Sociosexual knowledge, experience, attitudes, and interests of individuals with autistic disorder and developmental delay. *Journal of Autism and Developmental Disorders, 27*(4), 397–413. https://doi.org/10.1023/A:1025805405188

Kraemer, B., Delsignore, A., Gundelfinger, R., Schnyder, U., & Hepp, U. (2005). Comorbidity of Asperger syndrome and gender identity disorder. *European Child & Adolescent Psychiatry, 14* (5), 292–296. https://doi.org/10.1007/s00787-005-0469-4

Landén, M., & Rasmussen, P. (1997). Gender identity disorder in a girl with autism—a case report. *European Child & Adolescent Psychiatry, 6*(3), 170–173. https://doi.org/10.1007/BF00538990

Lemaire, M., Thomazeau, B., & Bonnet-Brilhault, F. (2014). Gender identity disorder and autism spectrum disorder in a 23-year-old female. *Archives of Sexual Behavior, 43*(2), 395–398. https://doi.org/10.1007/s10508-013-0141-x

Levac, D., Colquhoun, H., & O'Brien, K. K. (2010). Scoping studies: Advancing the methodology. *Implementation Science, 5*(1), 1–9. https://doi.org/10.1186/1748-5908-5-69

Lunsky, Y., & Konstantareas, M. M. (1998). The attitudes of individuals with autism and mental retardation towards sexuality. *Education and Training in Mental Retardation and Developmental Disabilities*, 24–33.

Mackin, M. L., Loew, N., Gonzalez, A., Tykol, H., & Christensen, T. (2016). Parent perceptions of sexual education needs for their children with autism. *Journal of Pediatric Nursing, 31*(6), 608–618. https://doi.org/10.1016/j.pedn.2016.07.003

May, T., Pang, K. C., O'Connell, M. A., & Williams, K. (2017). Typical pubertal timing in an Australian population of girls and boys with autism spectrum disorder. *Journal of Autism and Developmental Disorders, 47*(12), 3983–3993. https://doi.org/10.1007/s10803-017-3281-3

May, T., Pang, K. C., & Williams, K. (2017). Brief report: Sexual attraction and relationships in adolescents with autism. *Journal of Autism and Developmental Disorders, 47*(6), 1910–1916. https://doi.org/10.1007/s10803-017-3092-6

Mehzabin, P., & Stokes, M. A. (2011). Self-assessed sexuality in young adults with high-functioning autism. *Research in Autism Spectrum Disorders, 5*(1), 614–621. https://doi.org/10.1016/j.rasd.2010.07.006

Meister, C., Norlock, D., Honeyman, S., & Pierce, K. (1994). Sexuality and autism: A parenting skills enhancement group. *Canadian Journal of Human Sexuality, 3*(3), 283–289.

Milton, J., Duggan, C., Latham, A., Egan, V., & Tantam, D. (2002). Case history of co-morbid Asperger's syndrome and paraphilic behaviour. *Medicine, Science and the Law, 42*(3), 237–244. https://doi.org/10.1177/002580240204200308

Mogavero, M. C., & Hsu, K. H. (2019). Dating and courtship behaviors among those with autism spectrum disorder. *Sexuality and Disability*, 1–10. https://doi.org/10.1007/s11195-019-09565-8

Mukaddes, N. M. (2002). Gender identity problems in autistic children. *Child: Care, Health and Development, 28*(6), 529–532. https://doi.org/10.1046/j.1365-2214.2002.00301.x

Nichols, S., & Blakeley-Smith, A. (2009). "I'm not sure we're ready for this...": Working with families toward facilitating healthy sexuality for individuals with autism spectrum disorders. *Social Work in Mental Health, 8*(1), 72–91. https://doi.org/10.1080/15332980902932383

Øien, R. A., Cicchetti, D. V., & Nordahl-Hansen, A. (2018). Gender dysphoria, sexuality and autism spectrum disorders: A systematic map review. *Journal of Autism and Developmental Disorders, 48*(12), 4028–4037. https://doi.org/10.1007/s10803-018-3686-7

Orsmond, G. I., Krauss, M. W., & Seltzer, M. M. (2004). Peer relationships and social and recreational activities among adolescents and adults with autism. *Journal of Autism and Developmental Disorders, 34*(3), 245–256. https://doi.org/10.1023/B:JADD.0000029547.96610.df

Ousley, O. Y., & Mesibov, G. B. (1991). Sexual attitudes and knowledge of high-functioning adolescents and adults with autism. *Journal of Autism and Developmental Disorders, 21*(4), 471–481. https://doi.org/10.1007/BF02206871

Parchomiuk, M. (2019). Sexuality of persons with Autistic Spectrum Disorders (ASD). *Sexuality and Disability, 37*(2), 259–274. https://doi.org/10.1007/s11195-018-9534-z

Pasterski, V., Gilligan, L., & Curtis, R. (2014). Traits of autism spectrum disorders in adults with gender dysphoria. *Archives of Sexual Behavior, 43*(2), 387–393. https://doi.org/10.1007/s10508-013-0154-5

Pearlman-Avnion, S., Cohen, N., & Eldan, A. (2017). Sexual well-being and quality of life among high-functioning adults with autism. *Sexuality and Disability, 35*(3), 279–293. https://doi.org/10.1007/s11195-017-9490-z

Pecora, L. A., Mesibov, G. B., & Stokes, M. A. (2016). Sexuality in high-functioning autism: A systematic review and meta-analysis. *Journal of Autism and Developmental Disorders, 46*(11), 3519–3556. https://doi.org/10.1007/s10803-016-2892-4

Perera, H., Gadambanathan, T., & Weerasiri, S. (2011). Gender identity disorder presenting in a girl with Asperger's disorder and obsessive compulsive disorder. *Ceylon Medical Journal, 48*(2). https://doi.org/10.4038/cmj.v48i2.3374

Pryde, R., & Jahoda, A. (2018). A qualitative study of mothers' experiences of supporting the sexual development of their sons with autism and an accompanying intellectual disability. *International Journal of Developmental Disabilities, 64*(3), 166–174. https://doi.org/10.1080/20473869.2018.1446704

Qualls, L. R., Hartmann, K., & Paulson, J. F. (2018). Broad autism phenotypic traits and the relationship to sexual orientation and sexual behavior. *Journal of Autism and Developmental Disorders, 48*(12), 3974–3983. https://doi.org/10.1007/s10803-018-3556-3

Ray, F., Marks, C., & Bray-Garretson, H. (2004). Challenges to treating adolescents with Asperger's Syndrome who are sexually abusive. *Sexual Addiction & Compulsivity, 11*(4), 265–285. https://doi.org/10.1080/10720160490900614

Realmuto, G. M., & Ruble, L. A. (1999). Sexual behaviors in autism: Problems of definition and management. *Journal of Autism and Developmental Disorders, 29*(2), 121–127. https://doi.org/10.1023/A:1023088526314

Renty, J., & Roeyers, H. (2007). Individual and marital adaptation in men with autism spectrum disorder and their spouses: The role of social support and coping strategies. *Journal of Autism and Developmental Disorders, 37*(7), 1247–1255. https://doi.org/10.1007/s10803-006-0268-x

Roth, M. E., & Gillis, J. M. (2015). "Convenience with the Click of a Mouse": A survey of adults with autism spectrum disorder on online dating. *Sexuality and Disability, 33*(1), 133–150. https://doi.org/10.1007/s11195-014-9392-2

Ruble, L. A., & Dalrymple, N. J. (1993). Social/sexual awareness of persons with autism: A parental perspective. *Archives of Sexual Behavior, 22*(3), 229–240. https://doi.org/10.1007/BF01541768

Rudolph, C. E., Lundin, A., Åhs, J. W., Dalman, C., & Kosidou, K. (2018). Brief report: Sexual orientation in individuals with autistic traits: Population based study of 47,000 adults in Stockholm County. *Journal of Autism and Developmental Disorders, 48*(2), 619–624. https://doi.org/10.1007/s10803-017-3369-9

Sala, G., Hooley, M., Attwood, T., Mesibov, G. B., & Stokes, M. A. (2019). Autism and intellectual disability: A systematic review of sexuality and relationship education. *Sexuality and Disability, 37*(3), 353–382. https://doi.org/10.1007/s11195-019-09577-4

Schöttle, D., Briken, P., Tüscher, O., & Turner, D. (2017). Sexuality in autism: Hypersexual and paraphilic behavior in women and men with high-functioning autism spectrum disorder. *Dialogues in Clinical Neuroscience, 19*(4), 381–393.

Sevlever, M., Roth, M. E., & Gillis, J. M. (2013). Sexual abuse and offending in autism spectrum disorders. *Sexuality and Disability, 31*(2), 189–200. https://doi.org/10.1007/s11195-013-9286-8

Shumer, D. E., Reisner, S. L., Edwards-Leeper, L., & Tishelman, A. (2016). Evaluation of Asperger syndrome in youth presenting to a gender dysphoria clinic. *LGBT Health, 3*(5), 387–390. https://doi.org/10.1089/lgbt.2015.0070

Skagerberg, E., Di Ceglie, D., & Carmichael, P. (2015). Brief report: Autistic features in children and adolescents with gender dysphoria. *Journal of Autism and Developmental Disorders, 45*(8), 2628–2632. https://doi.org/10.1007/s10803-015-2413-x

Stokes, M., Newton, N., & Kaur, A. (2007). Stalking, and social and romantic functioning among adolescents and adults with autism spectrum disorder. *Journal of Autism and Developmental Disorders, 37*(10), 1969–1986. https://doi.org/10.1007/s10803-006-0344-2

Stokes, M. A., & Kaur, A. (2005). High-functioning autism and sexuality: A parental perspective. *Autism, 9*(3), 266–289. https://doi.org/10.1177/1362361305053258

Strang, J. F., Kenworthy, L., Dominska, A., Sokoloff, J., Kenealy, L. E., Berl, M., et al. (2014). Increased gender variance in autism spectrum disorders and attention deficit hyperactivity disorder. *Archives of Sexual Behavior, 43*(8), 1525–1533. https://doi.org/10.1007/s10508-014-0285-3

Strang, J. F., Powers, M. D., Knauss, M., Sibarium, E., Leibowitz, S. F., Kenworthy, L., et al. (2018). "They thought it was an obsession": Trajectories and perspectives of autistic transgender and gender-diverse adolescents. *Journal of Autism and Developmental Disorders, 48*(12), 4039–4055. https://doi.org/10.1007/s10803-018-3723-6

Strunz, S., Schermuck, C., Ballerstein, S., Ahlers, C. J., Dziobek, I., & Roepke, S. (2017). Romantic relationships and relationship satisfaction among adults with Asperger syndrome and high-functioning autism. *Journal of Clinical Psychology, 73*(1), 113–125. https://doi.org/10.1002/jclp.22319

Sullivan, A., & Caterino, L. C. (2008). Addressing the sexuality and sex education of individuals with autism spectrum disorders. *Education and Treatment of Children, 31*(3), 381–394.

Tarnai, B., & Wolfe, P. S. (2008). Social stories for sexuality education for persons with autism/pervasive developmental disorder. *Sexuality and Disability, 26*(1), 29–36. https://doi.org/10.1007/s11195-007-9067-3

Tateno, M., Tateno, Y., & Saito, T. (2008). Comorbid childhood gender identity disorder in a boy with Asperger syndrome. *Psychiatry and Clinical Neurosciences, 62*(2), 238–238. https://doi.org/10.1111/j.1440-1819.2008.01761.x

Torisky, C. (1985). Sex education and sexual awareness building for autistic children and youth: Some viewpoints and considerations. *Journal of Autism and Developmental Disorders, 15*(2), 213–227. https://doi.org/10.1007/BF01531607

Travers, J., & Tincani, M. (2010). Sexuality education for individuals with autism spectrum disorders: Critical issues and decision making guidelines. *Education and Training in Autism and Developmental Disabilities, 45*(2), 284–293.

Tullis, C. A., & Zangrillo, A. N. (2013). Sexuality education for adolescents and adults with autism spectrum disorders. *Psychology in the Schools, 50*(9), 866–875. https://doi.org/10.1002/pits.21713

van Bourgondien, M. E., Reichle, N. C., & Palmer, A. (1997). Sexual behavior in adults with autism. *Journal of Autism and Developmental Disorders, 27*(2), 113–125. https://doi.org/10.1023/A:1025883622452

van der Miesen, A. I., Hurley, H., Bal, A. M., & de Vries, A. L. (2018). Prevalence of the wish to be of the opposite gender in adolescents and adults with autism spectrum disorder. *Archives of Sexual Behavior, 47*(8), 2307–2317. https://doi.org/10.1007/s10508-018-1218-3

van der Miesen, A. I., Hurley, H., & De Vries, A. L. (2016). Gender dysphoria and autism spectrum disorder: A narrative review. *International Review of Psychiatry, 28*(1), 70–80. https://doi.org/10.3109/09540261.2015.1111199

van Schalkwyk, G. I., Klingensmith, K., & Volkmar, F. R. (2015). Gender identity and autism spectrum disorders. *The Yale Journal of Biology and Medicine, 88*(1), 81–83.

VanderLaan, D. P., Leef, J. H., Wood, H., Hughes, S. K., & Zucker, K. J. (2015). Autism spectrum disorder risk factors and autistic traits in gender dysphoric children. *Journal of Autism and Developmental Disorders, 45*(6), 1742–1750. https://doi.org/10.1007/s10803-014-2331-3

Violeta, K. J., & Langer, S. J. (2017). Integration of desire, sexual orientation, and female embodiment of a transgender woman previously diagnosed with autism spectrum disorder: A case report. *Journal of Gay & Lesbian Mental Health, 21*(4), 352–370. https://doi.org/10.1080/19359705.2017.1354794

Visser, K., Greaves-Lord, K., Tick, N. T., Verhulst, F. C., Maras, A., & van der Vegt, E. J. (2015). Study protocol: A randomized controlled trial investigating the effects of a psychosexual training program for adolescents with autism spectrum disorder. *BMC Psychiatry, 15*(1), 207. https://doi.org/10.1186/s12888-015-0586-7

Williams, P. G., Allard, A. M., & Sears, L. (1996). Case study: Cross-gender preoccupations in two male children with autism. *Journal of Autism and Developmental Disorders, 26*(6), 635–642. https://doi.org/10.1007/BF02172352

Wolfe, P. S., Condo, B., & Hardaway, E. (2009). Sociosexuality education for persons with autism spectrum disorders using principles of applied behavior analysis. *Teaching Exceptional Children, 42*(1), 50–61. https://doi.org/10.1177/004005990904200105

Chapter 3
Results

3.1 Study Characteristics

3.1.1 Year of Publication

To be included in this scoping review the study had to have been published between 1 January 2009 to 31 December 2019. In terms of publication year, no studies were published in 2009, 1 in 2010, 1 in 2011, 1 in 2012, 2 in 2013, 2 in 2014, 3 in 2015, 2 in 2016, 7 in 2017, 4 in 2018, and 4 in 2019 (see Table 3.1).

3.1.2 Location of the Study

In terms of the location in which the participants were recruited, in seven studies participants were recruited from the multiple countries, in four studies participants were recruited from the United States of America, three studies participants were recruited from Australia, six studies participants were recruited from the Netherlands, three studies participants were recruited from the United Kingdom of Great Britain and Northern Ireland, two studies participants were recruited from Israel, one study participants were recruited from Germany, and one study participants were recruited from Canada (see Table 3.1).

3.1.3 Sample Composition

In terms of sample size, van der Miesen et al. (2018) published the study that contained the largest sample of autistic participants; with 1380 participants (1085

Table 3.1 Study characteristics

Study	Autistic					Control sample					Country where participants were sampled
	M	F	Other	Age range (years)	Mean age (years)	M	F	Other	Age range (years)	Mean age (years)	
Barnett (2017)[a]	5	13	6	18–61	36.5						USA
Barnett and Maticka-Tyndale (2015)[a]				18–61	37						USA
Brown-Lavoie, Viecili, and Weiss (2014)[a]	58	36		19–43	27.83	66	51		18–35	27.60	USA, Canada
Bush (2019)[a]		248		18–30	23.2		179		18–30	21.8	USA, UK, Canada
Byers and Nichols (2014)[a]	77	128		21–62	38.6						USA, Australia, New Zealand, UK, Europe, Canada
Byers, Nichols, and Voyer (2013)[a]	61	68		21–73	35.3						USA, Australia, New Zealand, UK, Europe, Canada
Byers, Nichols, Voyer, and Reilly (2013)[a]	56	85									USA, Australia, New Zealand, UK, Europe, Canada
Cheak-Zamora, Teti, Maurer-Batjer, O'Connor, and Randolph (2019)[a]	20	7									USA
Cooper, Smith, and Russell (2018)[a]	118	101				148	153				UK
De Vries, Noens, Cohen-Kettenis, van Berckelaer-Onnes, and Doreleijers (2010)[a]	115	89			10.8						Netherlands
Dewinter, De Graaf, and Begeer (2017)[a]	326	349		15–80	43.2	3927	4137		15–70	42.64	Netherlands
Dewinter, Van Parys, Vermeiren, and Van Nieuwenhuizen (2017)[a]	8			16–20	17.87						Netherlands

Study											Country
Dewinter, Vermeiren, Vanwesenbeeck, and Van Nieuwenhuizen (2016)[a]	30		1	16.64–20.29	18.62	60		1	16.02–20.77	18.63	Netherlands and Belgium
Dewinter, Vermeiren, Vanwesenbeeck, Lobbestael, and Van Nieuwenhuizen (2015)[a]	50			15–18		90			15–18		Netherlands
Hancock, Stokes, and Mesibov (2019)[a]	96	135	1	14–56	25.13	66	160	1	13–59	22.16	UK
Hannah and Stagg (2016)[a]	12	8		18–25		7	13		18–25		Australia
May, Pang, and Williams (2017)[a]	73	21		14–15		1685	1675		14–15		North America, Europe, Australia
Mogavero and Hsu (2019)[a]	21	19	6	19–57	33.16	26	55	7	18–55	26.23	Israel
Pearlman-Avnion, Cohen, and Eldan (2017)[a]	18	11	2	17–62	27.79						Israel
Roth and Gillis (2015)[a]	6	11		19–50	29.59						USA
Strang et al. (2018)[a]	6	14	2	12.9–20.76	16.6						Germany
Strunz et al. (2017)[a]	92	137		18–58	34.9						Netherlands
van der Miesen, Hurley, Bal, and de Vries (2018)[a]	1085	295									Netherlands
George and Stokes (2018)[b]	90	219			31.01	103	158			30.20	Australia
Gilmour, Schalomo, and Smith (2012)[b]	27	55			28.90	102	180				Canada
Kanfiszer, Davies, and Collins (2017)[b]		7									UK
Mehzabin and Stokes (2011)[b]	12	9				15	24				Australia

Key: UK: The United Kingdom of Great Britain and Northern Ireland, USA: The United States of America

[a] Studies identified from the first phase of the search procedure

[b] Studies identified from the second phase of the search procedure

males; 295 females). In contrast, Kanfiszer et al. (2017) published the study that had the smallest sample of autistic participants (i.e., seven females). Barnett and Maticka-Tyndale (2015) did not report the number of participants in their study. In this scoping review 14 out of the 27 studies examined (51.85%) contained a control group. Dewinter, De Graaf, and Begeer (2017) published the study with the largest control group; 8064 participants (3927 males; 4137 females). In contrast, Hannah and Stagg (2016) published the study with the smallest control sample with 20 participants (7 males; 13 females) (see Table 3.1).

In terms of gender composition, three studies contained only samples of autistic males (Dewinter et al., 2015, 2016; Dewinter et al., 2017). Of these, the study with the largest sample was published by Dewinter et al. (2015); which had 50 autistic males. In contrast, Dewinter et al. (2017) published the study with the smallest sample of autistic males (i.e., eight males). Two studies contained only samples of autistic females (Bush, 2019; Kanfiszer et al., 2017). Bush (2019) published the study with the largest sample; which had 248 autistic females. In contrast, Kanfiszer et al. (2017) published the study with the smallest sample of autistic females (i.e., 7 females). Out of the 28 studies examined, 22 (78.57%) contained mixed samples of both autistic males and autistic females. Van der Miesen et al. (2018) published the study with the largest mixed sample (1085 males; 295 females). In contrast, Roth and Gillis (2015) published the study with the smallest mixed sample (6 males; 11 females). One study did not specify the gender composition of their sample of autistics (Barnett & Maticka-Tyndale, 2015). Collectively, across the 28 studies examined, 4853 autistic participants (2552 males; 2284 females; 17 other) and 13,315 non-autistic participants (6364 males; 6943 females; 8 other) were examined (see Table 3.1).

In terms of age composition, 10 of the 28 studies examined (35.71%) contained only samples of autistic adults (i.e., those aged over 18 years), two studies (7.14%) contained only samples of autistic children (i.e., those younger than 18 years of age), and six studies (21.42%) contained mixed samples of autistic children and autistic adults. However, nine studies (32.14%) did not report the age range of the autistic participants sampled. Thus, it was not possible to conclude if they contained samples of only autistic children, samples of only autistic adults, or samples of both autistic children and autistic adults. Out of the 10 studies in which autistic adults were only sampled, the study with the largest number of participants was published by Bush (2019) (i.e., 248 autistic adults) while the study with the smallest sample of autistic adults was published by Roth and Gillis (2015) (i.e., 17 autistic adults). De Vries et al. (2010) published the study with the largest number of autistic children (i.e., 204 autistic children) while May et al. (2017) published the study with the smallest number of autistic children (i.e., 94 children). Out of the six studies which had mixed samples of both adults and children, the study with the largest number of participants was published by Dewinter, De Graaf, and Begeer (2017), which contained 675 participants (326 males; 349 females) and 8064 non-autistic participants (3927 males; 4137 females). In contrast, the study with the smallest number of adult and children participants was published by Dewinter et al. (2017), which contained eight autistic participants (8 males) (see Table 3.1).

3.2   Sexual Orientation

Out of the 27 studies examined, fourteen (51.85%) documented the sexual orientation of the autistic participants (Barnett & Maticka-Tyndale, 2015; Barnett, 2017; Brown-Lavoie et al., 2014; Bush, 2019; Byers & Nichols, 2014; Byers, Nichols, Voyer, & Reilly, 2013; Byers, Nichols, & Voyer, 2013; Cooper et al., 2018; Dewinter, De Graaf, & Begeer, 2017; Fernandes et al., 2016; May et al., 2017; Mogavero & Hsu, 2019; Roth & Gillis, 2015; Strunz et al., 2017). Of these, four compared the proportion of different sexual orientations within a sample of autistics against a sample of allistic participants (i.e., a control group) (Cooper et al., 2018; Dewinter, De Graaf, & Begeer, 2017; May et al., 2017; Mogavero & Hsu, 2019). The other ten studies did not include a control group since they only measured the proportion of different sexual orientations within autistic samples (Barnett & Maticka-Tyndale, 2015; Barnett, 2017; Brown-Lavoie et al., 2014; Bush, 2019; Byers & Nichols, 2014; Byers, Nichols, Voyer, & Reilly, 2013; Byers, Nichols, & Voyer, 2013; Fernandes et al., 2016; Roth & Gillis, 2015; Strunz et al., 2017) (see Table 3.2).

3.2.1   Asexuality

Asexuality is conceptualised as a unique sexual orientation, widely accepted as meaning a lack of sexual attraction to other people (Brotto & Yule, 2017). Six studies documented the rates of asexuality within autistic samples (Barnett, 2017; Barnett & Maticka-Tyndale, 2015; Bush, 2019; Dewinter, De Graaf, & Begeer, 2017; May et al., 2017; Roth & Gillis, 2015). Of these, two compared the rates of asexuality between a sample of autistics and a sample of non-autistics (Dewinter, De Graaf, & Begeer, 2017; May et al., 2017). The other four studies only documented rates of asexuality among samples of autistics (Barnett, 2017; Barnett & Maticka-Tyndale, 2015; Bush, 2019; Roth & Gillis, 2015). Barnett and Maticka-Tyndale (2015), and Barnett (2017) stated that 25% of their samples of autistics identified as asexual. Bush (2019) stated that 13% of their sample said they were asexual. Finally, Roth and Gillis (2015) stated that 6% of their sample of autistic participants disclosed that they were bisexual. Unlike other studies about this topic, Dewinter, De Graaf, and Begeer (2017) and May et al. (2017) compared the rates of asexuality between their autistic and non-autistic samples. Dewinter, De Graff, and Begeer documented greater rates of asexuality in the sample of autistic females (14.9%) than in the sample of non-autistic females (1.6%). Dewinter, De Graff, and Begeer also claimed that asexuality was more common in their sample of autistic males (4.7%) than in their sample of non-autistic males (1.1%). May, Pang, and Williams reported that the same proportion of asexuality (5%) was measured in their samples of autistic and non-autistic females. In contrast, May, Pang, and Williams claimed that asexuality was more common in their sample of autistic males (9%) than in their sample of non-autistic males (3%). Collectively, these six studies show that asexuality was

Table 3.2 Sexual orientation status of participants in the examined studies

Study	Autistic participants n (% of total sample)	Typically developing (TD) group n (% of total sample)
Barnett and Maticka-Tyndale (2015)	Asexual 6 (25%) Bisexual 4 (17%) Heterosexual 11 (45%) Lesbian/gay 3 (13%)	
Barnett (2017)	Asexual 6 (25%) Heterosexual 74 (79%) Lesbian, gay, or queer 7 (29%)	
Brown-Lavoie et al. (2014)	Heterosexual 74 (79%) Lesbian, gay, bisexual 20 (21%)	
Bush (2019)	Asexual 32 (13%) Bisexual 30 (12%) Heterosexual 20 (8%) Pansexual or polysexual 30 (12%) Queer 25 (10%)	
Byers and Nichols (2014)	Bisexual 49 (23%) Heterosexual 156 (77%)	
Byers, Nichols, and Voyer (2013)	Bisexual 12 (9%) Heterosexual 75 (58%) Lesbian, gay, or homosexual 19 (15%) Unlabelled 16 (12%) Unsure 7 (5%)	
Byers, Nichols, Voyer, and Reilly (2013)	Bisexual 17 (12%) Heterosexual 96 (68%) Unknown/other 28 (20%)	
Cooper et al. (2018)	*Autistic female group (n = 101)* Heterosexual 32 (31%) Homosexual 69 (68%) *Autistic male group (n = 118)* Heterosexual 74 (63%) Homosexual 44 (37%)	*TD female group* *(n = 153)* Heterosexual 127 (84%) Homosexual 26 (16%) *TD male group (n = 114)* Heterosexual 90 (79%) Homosexual 24 (21%)
Dewinter, De Graaf, and Begeer (2017)	*Autistic female group (n = 343)* Asexual 51 (14.9%) Bisexual 77 (22.4%) Heterosexual 194 (56.6%) Lesbian 21 (6.1%) *Autistic male group (n = 316)* Asexual 15 (4.7%) Bisexual 27 (8.5%) Gay 16 (5.1%) Heterosexual 258 (81.6%)	*TD female group* *(n = 4137)* Asexual 65 (1.6%) Bisexual 418 (10.1%) Heterosexual 3601 (87%) Lesbian 53 (1.3%) *TD male group (n = 3927)* Asexual 44 (1.1%) Bisexual 184 (4.7%) Gay 150 (3.8%) Heterosexual 3549 (90.4%)

(continued)

Table 3.2 (continued)

Study	Autistic participants n (% of total sample)	Typically developing (TD) group n (% of total sample)
Fernandes et al. (2016)	*Study 1 (n = 65)* Bisexual* Heterosexual 39 (60%) Homosexual 19 (29%) Unknown 7 (11%) *Study 2 (n = 55)* Bisexual 3 (5%) Heterosexual 49 (89%) Homosexual 3 (5%) Unknown 0 (0%)	
May et al. (2017)	*Autistic female group (n = 18)* Asexual 1 (5%) Bisexual 5 (27%) Heterosexual 9 (47%) Lesbian 0 (0%) Unknown 3 (21%) *Autistic male group (n = 59)* Asexual 6 (9%) Bisexual 3 (5%) Gay 0 (0%) Heterosexual 49 (82%) Unknown 1 (3%)	*TD female group (n = 1600)* Asexual 77 (5%) Bisexual 66 (4%) Heterosexual 1369 (86%) Lesbian 20 (1%) Unknown 68 (4%) *TD male group (n = 1627)* Asexual 53 (3%) Bisexual 31 (2%) Gay 6 (0.4%) Heterosexual 1509 (93%) Unknown 28 (1%)
Mogavero and Hsu (2019)	Bisexual 2 (4.3%) Declined to answer 6 (13%) Heterosexual 28 (60.9%) Lesbian/gay 4 (8.7%) Other 6 (13%)	Bisexual 6 (6.8%) Declined to answer 7 (15.2%) Heterosexual 72 (81.8%) Lesbian/gay 2 (2.3%) Other 1 (1.1%)
Roth and Gillis (2015)	Asexual 1 (6%) Bisexual 3 (17%) Heterosexual 10 (59%) Lesbian/gay 2 (12%) Pansexual 1 (6%)	
Strunz et al. (2017)	Bisexual 22 (10%) Heterosexual 159 (69%) Homosexual 17 (7%) Not disclosed 31 (14%)	

Key: * was not asked

more common in the autistic population than the non-autistic population, although the rates varied between the studies (see Table 3.2).

3.2.2 Bisexuality

Flanders et al. (2017, p. 39) suggest that *"bisexuality is defined in a plethora of ways, including definitions based on behavior, attraction, or desire and may employ binary or nonbinary definitions"*. This can complicate the collection of quantitative data on bisexuality as each study or individual within the study may have a slightly different interpretation of what bisexuality is and therefore if they would or would not categorise themselves as bisexual. For example, some researchers focus on bisexuality as the existence of attraction to more than one gender, or specifically to both men and women, whilst others say that in order to meet the criteria for bisexual an individual must have sexual or relationship behaviour with more than one gender, (Rosenthal, Sylva, Safron, & Bailey, 2011). When gender diverse individuals are identifying their sexual orientation, some may identify as pan or omni-sexual, whilst others with similar sexual attraction and desire patterns may identify as bisexual.

Ten studies documented the proportion of autistics in their samples who identified as being bisexual (Barnett & Maticka-Tyndale, 2015; Bush, 2019; Byers & Nichols, 2014; Byers, Nichols, & Voyer, 2013; Byers, Nichols, Voyer, & Reilly, 2013; Dewinter, De Graaf, & Begeer, 2017; Fernandes et al., 2016; May et al., 2017; Mogavero & Hsu, 2019; Strunz et al., 2017). Of these, three studies contained both an autistic and a non-autistic sample (Dewinter, De Graaf, & Begeer, 2017; May et al., 2017; Mogavero & Hsu, 2019) and seven studies only contained a sample of autistics (Barnett & Maticka-Tyndale, 2015; Bush, 2019; Byers & Nichols, 2014; Byers, Nichols, & Voyer, 2013; Byers, Nichols, Voyer, & Reilly, 2013; Fernandes et al., 2016; Strunz et al., 2017) (see Table 3.2).

In terms of studies that only contained samples of autistics, Barnett and Maticka-Tyndale (2015), Bush (2019), Byers and Nichols (2014), Byers, Nichols, and Voyer (2013), Byers, Nichols, Voyer, and Reilly (2013), Fernandes et al. (2016), and Strunz et al. (2017) all reported rates of bisexuality within their autistic samples (17%, 13%, 23%, 9%, 12%, 5%, and 10% respectfully). While these studies did not contain a control group, the rates documented are greater than what has been traditionally reported in studies about bisexuality in the general population (1–2%) (Savin-Williams & Cohen, 2018) (see Table 3.2).

Three studies compared the rates of bisexuality in a sample of autistics and in a sample of non-autistics (Dewinter, De Graaf, & Begeer, 2017; May et al., 2017; Mogavero & Hsu, 2019). Dewinter, De Graaf, and Begeer (2017) reported that bisexuality was more common in their samples of autistic females (22.4%) and autistic males (8.5%) than in their samples of non-autistic females (10.1%) and non-autistic males (4.7%). May et al. (2017) stated that bisexuality was more common among their samples of autistic females (27%) and autistic males (5%) than in their samples of non-autistic females (4%) and non-autistic males (2%). Unlike these studies, Mogavero and Hsu (2019) reported that bisexuality was more common in their non-autistic sample (6.5%) than in their sample of autistics (4.3%) (see Table 3.2).

3.2.3   *Homosexuality*

Roughgarden (2017) discussed the evolution of the definition of homosexuality, from same-sex sexual behaviours, through same-sex attracted to a personal identity. As with bisexuality, the lack of a consensus clear definition can lead to a level of inaccuracy in data collection. A person who has not had any sexual experiences may be reluctant to label themselves homosexual, whilst another who has had homosexual experiences but lives somewhere where that is illegal, may also be reluctant to describe themselves as homosexual. In the past, the focus was on same-sex sexual behaviours, seen as a mental illness in the *Diagnostic and Statistical Manual of Mental Disorders* (DSM) until 1973 and pathologized in the *International Statistical Classification of Diseases and Related Health Problems* (ICD) until 1991 (Mundle, Mahler, & Bhugra, 2015). Homosexuality is more currently understood as a sexual orientation reflecting same-sex attraction with male-male attracted people often being described as gay and female-female attracted people being described as lesbian.

Nine studies described the proportion of homosexuality in their samples of autistics (Barnett & Maticka-Tyndale, 2015; Barnett, 2017; Brown-Lavoie et al., 2014; Byers, Nichols, & Voyer, 2013; Cooper et al., 2018; Fernandes et al., 2016; Mogavero & Hsu, 2019; Roth & Gillis, 2015; Strunz et al., 2017). These studies did not offer a breakdown of male homosexuality (i.e., gay) or female homosexuality (i.e., lesbian). All studies that measured the proportion of homosexuality in the autistic population showed that it is more common among autistics than non-autistics. Out of these nine studies, seven reported rates of homosexuality in only samples of autistics (Barnett & Maticka-Tyndale, 2015; Barnett, 2017; Brown-Lavoie et al., 2014; Byers, Nichols, & Voyer, 2013; Fernandes et al., 2016; Roth & Gillis, 2015; Strunz et al., 2017), and two compared rates of homosexuality between samples of autistics and non-autistics (Cooper et al., 2018; Mogavero & Hsu, 2019) (see Table 3.2).

In terms of studies that only measured homosexuality among samples of autistics, Barnett and Maticka-Tyndale (2015), Barnett (2017), Brown-Lavoie et al. (2014), Byers, Nichols, and Voyer (2013), Roth and Gillis (2015), and Strunz et al. (2017) reported the percentage of their autistic sample that identified as homosexual (13%, 29%, 21%, 15%, 12%, and 7% respectfully) (see Table 3.2).

Cooper et al. (2018) and Mogavero and Hsu (2019) compared the proportion of homosexuality in a sample of autistics and a sample of non-autistics. Cooper, Smith, and Russell reported that homosexuality was more common in their sample of autistic males (37%) and autistic females (68%) than in their samples of non-autistic males (21%) and non-autistic females (16%). Mogavero and Hsu reported that homosexuality was more common in their autistic sample (8.7%) than in their non-autistic sample (2.3%) (see Table 3.2).

3.2.4   Lesbian

Two studies compare the proportions of lesbianism between samples of autistics and non-autistics (Dewinter, De Graaf, & Begeer, 2017; May et al., 2017). Dewinter, De Graaf, and Begeer (2017) found that 6.1% of autistics identified as being lesbians as opposed to 1.3% of non-autistics. In May et al.'s (2017) study no autistics identified as a lesbian and 20 non-autistics (1%) identified as lesbians (see Table 3.2).

3.2.5   Gay

Two studies compared the proportion of autistics and non-autistics who identified as gay (Dewinter, De Graaf, & Begeer, 2017; May et al., 2017). Dewinter, De Graaf, and Begeer (2017) stated that male homosexuality was more common in their sample of autistics (5.1%) than in their sample of non-autistics (3.8%). In another study, May et al. (2017) claimed that no autistics in their study identified as gay while 6 (0.4%) of non-autistics identified as gay (see Table 3.2).

3.2.6   Pansexuality and Polysexuality

Pansexuality is a sexual orientation in which a person is sexually and/or romantically attracted towards someone regardless of his or her biological sex or gender identity. In contrast, polysexuality is a state of being attracted towards multiple genders. Two studies documented the proportion of their autistic samples that identified as pansexual (Bush, 2019; Roth & Gillis, 2015). Bush (2019) reported that 12% of their sample of autistics disclosed that they were either pansexual or polysexual. Roth and Gillis (2015) stated that in their sample of autistic participants 6% disclosed that they were pansexual (see Table 3.2).

3.2.7   Heterosexuality

Heterosexuality is the sexual orientation referring to opposite sex attracted individuals. Four studies compared the proportion of heterosexuality between samples of autistics and non-autistics (Cooper et al., 2018; Dewinter, De Graaf, & Begeer, 2017; May et al., 2017; Mogavero & Hsu, 2019). Cooper et al. (2018) reported that non-autistic males and non-autistic females had a greater likelihood of being heterosexual (79% and 84% respectfully) than autistic males and autistic females (63% and 31% respectfully). In their study, Dewinter, De Graaf, and Begeer (2017) claimed that greater rates of heterosexuality were measured in their samples of non-autistic males and non-autistic females (90.4% and 87% respectfully) than autistic males and autistic females (81.6% and 56.6% respectfully). May et al. (2017) found that heterosexuality was disclosed more often among non-autistic females and non-autistic males (86% and 93% respectfully) than autistic males and autistic females (82% and 47% respectfully). Finally, Mogavero and Hsu (2019) claimed that heterosexuality was more common among non-autistics (81.8%) than among their autistic counterparts (60.9%) (see Table 3.2).

3.3   Gender Identity

Gender identity in Western cultures has had significant shifts in the last few decades, going from a mainly binary male/female construct, despite approximately one percent of live births being children who are intersex. Intersex individuals are born with both male and female biological characteristics. A binary and fixed conceptualization of gender still predominates Western thinking about gender, although the last twenty years have seen a growing awareness of gender variance and variability (Losty & O'Connor, 2018). This is in direct contrast to many traditional cultures which have more than two binary genders, with cultural norms for all genders.

Eight studies documented the gender identity that the autistic participants identified (Barnett & Maticka-Tyndale, 2015; Barnett, 2017; Bush, 2019; Cooper et al., 2018; Dewinter, De Graaf, & Begeer, 2017; George & Stokes, 2018; Mogavero & Hsu, 2019; Pearlman-Avnion et al., 2017). Of these, three compared the proportion of diverse gender identities of autistic participants to non-autistic peers (Cooper et al., 2018; George & Stokes, 2018; Mogavero & Hsu, 2019), and five studies solely measured different types of gender identity in samples of autistic participants (Barnett, 2017; Barnett & Maticka-Tyndale, 2015; Bush, 2019; Dewinter, De Graaf, & Begeer, 2017; Pearlman-Avnion et al., 2017). Dewinter, De Graaf, and Begeer's (2017) study contained the largest sample of autistic participants (i.e., 675 participants). George and Stokes (2018) published a study with the largest group of autistic and typically developing participants, with 309 and 261 participants respectfully (see Table 3.3).

Four studies documented the proportion of the autistic sample that identified as having a diverse gender type (Barnett, 2017; Barnett & Maticka-Tyndale, 2015; Bush, 2019; Dewinter, De Graaf, & Begeer, 2017). Barnett (2017) claimed that 25% of their sample of autistics (i.e., 6 out of 24 participants) revealed that they were either *'Androgynous, transgender, or genderqueer'*. Barnett and Maticka-Tyndale (2015) stated that 21% of their sample of autistics (i.e., 6 out of 24 participants) claimed that they were either *'androgynous or genderqueer'*. Dewinter, De Graaf, and Begeer (2017) found that 7.4% of autistic females surveyed (i.e., 26 out of 349 participants) and 0.6% of autistic males (i.e., 2 out of 326 participants) identified as androgynous. Finally, Bush (2019) documented that 17% of their autistic sample identified as androgynous. None of these studies contained a control group. Thus, it

Table 3.3 Gender identify status of participants in the examined studies

Study	Autistic participants n (% of total sample)	Typically developing (TD) group n (% of total sample)
Barnett and Maticka-Tyndale (2015)	Androgynous or genderqueer 5 (21%) Cisman 6 (25%) Ciswoman 13 (54%)	
Barnett (2017)	Androgynous, Transgender, or genderqueer 6 (25%) Cisman 5 (21%) Ciswoman 13 (54%)	
Bush (2019)	"Demigirl" or somewhat but not entirely feminine (7%) Androgynous (17%) Genderfluid, or experiencing fluctuation in the extent to which one identifies as masculine, feminine, or other genders (4%) Genderqueer or non-binary or not identifying as exclusively masculine or feminine and/or not ascribing to traditional gender roles, expectations, and stereotypes (15%)	
Cooper et al. (2018)	*Autistic female group (n = 101)* Cisfemale 67 (66%) Identify as other gender 34 (34%) *Autistic male group (n = 118)* Cismale 105 (89%) Identify as other gender 13 (11%)	*TD female group (n = 153)* Cisfemale 149 (97%) Identify as other gender 4 (3%) *TD male group (n = 114)* Cismale 108 (95%) Identify as other gender 6 (5%)
Dewinter, De Graaf, and Begeer (2017)	*Autistic female group (n = 349)* Androgynous 26 (7.4%) Feels male 3 (0.9%) Different (e.g., human, no sex) 8 (2.3%) Don't know (yet) 9 (2.6%) Cisfemale 272 (77.9%) Partly male, partly female 31 (8.9%) *Autistic male group (n = 326)* Androgynous 2 (0.6%) Cismale 299 (91.7%) Different (e.g., human, no sex) 8 (2.5%) Don't know (yet) 4 (1.2)	

(continued)

Table 3.3 (continued)

Study	Autistic participants n (% of total sample)	Typically developing (TD) group n (% of total sample)
	Feels female 3 (0.9%) Partly male, partly female 10 (3.1%)	
Mogavero and Hsu (2019)	Cisfemale 19 (41.3%) Cismale 21 (45.7%) Transgender/non-binary 6 (13%)	Cisfemale 55 (62.5%) Cismale 26 (29.5%) Transgender/non-binary 7 (8%)
Pearlman-Avnion et al. (2017)	Cisfemale 11 (35%) Cismale 18 (58%) Other 2 (6%)	
George and Stokes (2018)	*Autistic female group (n = 219)* Bigendered 7 (3.3%) Ciswoman 147 (62.1%) Cross-dresser 0 (0%) Genderqueer 26 (12%) Male 5 (2.3%) Other 29 (13.4%) Transgender 5 (2.3%) *Autistic male group (n = 90)* Bigendered 2 (2.2%) Cismale 69 (77.8%) Cross-dresser 1 (1.1%) Genderqueer 1 (1.1%) Other 3 (3.3%) Transgender 7 (7.8%) Woman 7 (7.8%)	*TD female group (n = 158)* Bigendered 6 (3.8%) Ciswoman 138 (87.3%) Cross-dresser 0 (0%) Genderqueer 8 (5.1%) Male 2 (1.3%) Other 3 (1.9%) Transgender 1 (0.6%) *TD male group (n = 103)* Bigendered 1 (1%) Cismale 96 (93.1%) Cross-dresser 0 (0%) Genderqueer 0 (0%) Other 2 (2%) Transgender 4 (3.9%) Woman 0 (0%)

was not possible to compare rates of androgyny among the autistic samples to such rates in samples of non-autistic participants. However, autistics are more inclined to identify as androgynous when the results from these studies are compare to the results in studies about the rates of androgyny among members of the general population (1%) (Stotzer, Ka'opua, & Diaz, 2014) (see Table 3.3).

Three studies measured the proportion of the autistic sample who identified as transgender (Barnett, 2017; George & Stokes, 2018; Mogavero & Hsu, 2019). Of these, one sampled exclusively autistics (Barnett, 2017) and two sampled a group of autistics and a control group (George & Stokes, 2018; Mogavero & Hsu, 2019). Mogavero and Hsu (2019) found that six out of forty-six autistics in their study (13%) disclosed that they were transgender/non-binary while seven out of eighty-eight participants in their control group (8%) identified as transgender/non-binary. George and Stokes (2018) indicated that autistic males revealed greater rates of transgenderism than those in the non-autistic male control group (7.8% and 3.9% respectfully). Additionally, George and Stokes also claimed that autistic females disclosed greater rates of transgenderism than those in the non-autistic female control group (2.3% and 0.6% respectfully). The results from George and Stokes (2018), and Mogavero and Hsu (2019) found that there is a larger proportion of transgenderism within the autistic population than the non-autistic population. Finally, six out of twenty-four participants (25%) in Barnett's (2017) study disclosed that they were either androgynous, transgender, or genderqueer (see Table 3.3).

There are studies about autistics and their experiences of gender dysphoria. In 2018, Strang and colleagues documented the gender dysphoria experiences of twenty-two autistics who were diagnosed with gender dysphoria. Among other recollections, the participants' described the earliest time in their life when they had identified as gender nonconforming, a description of their initial thoughts about their gender nonconformity, and the point in time when they first felt that they might be comfortable being the opposite gender. Eight of the twenty-two participants recalled that during elementary school they had their first inclination of their gender nonconformity. Additionally, seven out of the twenty-two participants explained that the earliest self-acknowledgement of their gender nonconformity occurred when they *"felt more comfortable being with or associating with people of the other gender"*. Finally, nine out of twenty-two participants disclosed that the first point in their life when they might have felt that they might be another gender occurred when they were in middle school.

3.4   Sexual Relationships

3.4.1   *Relationships in General*

Five studies documented the relationship status of autistics (Dewinter, De Graaf, & Begeer, 2017; May et al., 2017; Mogavero & Hsu, 2019; Pearlman-Avnion et al., 2017; Strunz et al., 2017). Of these, three compared the relationship status of a sample of autistics to a sample of non-autistics (Dewinter, De Graaf, & Begeer, 2017; May et al., 2017; Mogavero & Hsu, 2019) and two studies only documented the relationship status of a sample of autistic participants (Pearlman-Avnion et al., 2017; Strunz et al., 2017) (see Table 3.4).

Table 3.4 Relationship status

Study	Autistic participants n (% of total sample)	Typically developing (TD) group n (% of total sample)
Dewinter, De Graaf, and Begeer (2017)	*Autistic male group (n = 316, 100%)* In a relationship (n = 158, 50%) With a man (n = 8, 2.5%) With a woman (n = 150, 47.5%) *Autistic female group (n = 343, 100%)* In a relationship (n = 162, 47.2%) With a man (n = 151, 44%) With a woman (n = 11, 3.2%)	*TD male group (n = 3927, 100%)* In a relationship (n = 2916, 74.3%) With a man (n = 113, 2.9%) With a woman (n = 2803, 71.4%) *TD female group (4137, 100%)* In a relationship (n = 2923, 70.7%) With a man (n = 2861, 69.2%) With a woman (n = 62, 1.5%)
May et al. (2017)	*Autistic male group (n = 61, 100%)* In a relationship (n = 7, 11%) Not in a relationship (n = 54, 89%) *TD male group (n = 1685, 100%)* In a relationship (n = 253, 15%) Not in a relationship (n = 1432, 85%)	*Autistic female group (n = 19, 100%)* In a relationship (n = 4, 20%) Not in a relationship (n = 15, 80%) *TD female group (n = 1675, 100%)* In a relationship (n = 268, 16%) Not in a relationship (n = 1407, 84%)
Pearlman-Avnion et al. (2017)	*Autistic sample (n = 31, 100%)* In a relationship (n = 14, 45.2%) Not in a relationship (n = 17, 54.8%)	
Mogavero and Hsu (2019)	*Autistic sample (n = 46, 100%)* In a relationship (n = 19, 41.3%) Not in a relationship (n = 27, 58.6%)	*TD sample (88, 100%)* In a relationship (n = 53, 60.2%) Not in a relationship (n = 35, 39.8%)
Strunz et al. (2017)	*Autistic females (n = 137, 100%)* In a relationship (n = 66, 48%) Not in a relationship (n = 71, 52%) *Autistic males (92, 100%)* In a relationship (n = 34, 37%) Not in a relationship (n = 58, 63%)	

May et al. (2017) and Mogavero and Hsu (2019) compared the relationship status of a sample of autistics and a sample of non-autistics. May et al. found that non-autistic males were more likely to be in a relationship than autistic males, 15% and 11% respectfully. However, non-autistic females were less likely to be in a relationship than autistic females, 16% and 20% respectfully. Mogavero and Hsu found that non-autistic participants were more inclined to be in a relationship than autistic participants (60.2% vs. 41.3% respectfully). Mogavero and Hsu documented the length and number of previous relationships that the autistic participants had experienced. They reported that 22 participants (48.9%) had a previous relationship of less than one year, four participants (8.9%) had a pervious relationship of between one to two years, and 19 participants (42.4%) had a pervious relationship of more than two years. In terms of a number of relationships, 9 participants (19.6%) did not report ever experiencing a relationship, 6 participants (13%) reported experiencing one previous relationship, 14 participants (30.4%) reported experiencing between two to three previous relationships, and 17 participants (37%) disclosed that they had experienced four or more previous relationships (see Table 3.4).

Pearlman-Avnion et al. (2017) and Strunz et al. (2017) documented the proportion of their sample of autistics that were in a relationship at the time of the study. However, these studies did not incorporate into their research design a control group. Pearlman-Avnion et al. found that most of the autistic participants in their study were not in a relationship (n = 17, 54.8%) and Strunz et al. reported that most autistic males (n = 58, 63%) and most autistic females (n = 71, 52%) in their study disclosed that they were not in a relationship. Strunz and colleagues also documented the reasons that 129 autistic participants who were single gave for not being in a relationship. The most common reason articulated was that *"contact with others was too exhausting"* (n = 84, 65%). In contrast, the least cited reason was *"I simply don't feel the need for a romantic relationship"* (n = 24, 19%) (see Table 3.4).

Unlike other studies, Dewinter, De Graaf, and Begeer (2017) compared the proportion of autistics and non-autistic participants that were in a relationship along with their types of relationships. They reported that non-autistic males (74.3%) and non-autistic females (70.7%) were more inclined to be in a relationship compared to autistic males (50%) and autistic females (47.4%). Non-autistic males were more inclined to be in a heterosexual (71.4% vs 47.5%) or a homosexual (2.9% vs 2.5%) relationship. Non-autistic females were more likely to be in a heterosexual relationship than autistic females, 69.2% and 44% respectfully. However, autistic females were more inclined to be in a homosexual relationship than non-autistic females, 3.2% and 1.5% respectfully (see Table 3.4).

3.5   Online Sexual Activities

3.5.1   *Learning About Sexual Issues Online*

Several studies have described the methods and sources that autistics have used to obtain knowledge about socially and culturally appropriate sexual behaviours and relationships. Dewinter et al. (2017) reported that autistic boys have obtained this knowledge from interactions with their parents and teachers, from remarks and jokes made by their peers, and from information they sourced from the internet. However, these autistic boys admitted that accompanying these different sources were challenges around obtaining accurate and appropriate sexual information. For instance, out of the eight autistic boys who participated in Dewinter et al.'s study, only one (i.e., Neville) felt comfortable communicating about issues concerning sexuality with their parents. The other boys reported that their parents had judgemental attitudes that prevented them from openly asking for information about sexual behaviours and relationships. Similarly, six of the eight autistic boys explained that they viewed pornography on the internet to get aroused. However, they all understood that while these pornographic sex scenes were unrealistic, they did provide a good starting point to obtain additional information. This sentiment was articulated by Andy, who stated:

> You first look at the image you see, for instance in porn . . . it might be fantasy so you want to know how it is for real . . . so you look for information (Dewinter et al., 2017, p. 79).

Brown-Lavoie et al. (2014) have also described the sources of information that autistics access to learn about sexual behaviours and relationships. Unlike Dewinter et al. (2017), which used interpretative phenomenological analysis to examine qualitative data, they reported statistical information about this topic. They compared the sources of information that autistics and non-autistics accessed to learn about sexually transmitted infections (STIs), appropriate sexual behaviours, and contraception. Their results were based on a sample of 94 autistics (58 males; 36 females) and 117 non-autistics (66 males; 51 females). They found that most autistics obtained information about sexual health from the internet (n = 51, 54.3%) while non-autistic predominantly obtained this information from their teachers (n = 72, 61.5%). Regarding appropriate sexual behaviours, they found that autistics (n = 66, 70.2%) and non-autistics (n = 67, 57.3%) predominantly learnt about these behaviours from the internet. Finally, autistics often accessed the internet to learn about contraception (n = 54, 57.4%) while non-autistics talked to their teachers (n = 65, 55.5%). Due to these results, Brown-Lavoie, Viecili, and Weiss concluded that autistics tend to use non-social sources of information (i.e., the internet) to earn about sexual health and contraception than their non-autistic counterpart who instead use social sources (i.e., their teachers).

3.5.2   Online Dating

Aside from acquiring sexual knowledge, autistics have also used the internet as a means to find their partners. Although not a big statistical difference, Dewinter et al. (2016) reported that autistics tended to use the internet to find a suitable partner (n = 2, 6.7%) slightly more than non-autistics (n = 3, 5%). In another study, Roth and Gillis (2015) found that slightly more than half of the autistic participants they sampled (n = 9, 53%) had used an online dating service. Those who used such a service reported using them on average for 4.37 years and had an average of 7.13 dates. In comparison to traditional face-to-face dating practices, six participants (46%) claimed that online dating was easier, three participants (23%) claimed that online dating was more difficult, and four participants (23%) claimed that there was no difference in complexity between online and face-to-face dating practices.

In conjunction with presenting statistical information, Roth and Gillis also presented their autistic participants' insights about the benefits and drawbacks of online dating services. They found that the most common benefit of using these services were the convenience of available information about the other partner. For example, one participant stated, *"reading about the other person to judge if I want to talk to them is easier then approaching people and trying to judge their body language or know what questions to ask"* (Roth & Gillis, 2015, p. 138). On the flipside, the most commonly cited drawback was being safe online. As noted by one participant *"troublesome especially for Aspies as [we] tend to be a bit naïve and frustrating"* (Roth & Gillis, 2015, p. 139). To mitigate these safety concerns, participants used several strategies that maintained their safety and anonymity online, such as withholding information that could be used to identify them (e.g., age or residential location).

Dewinter et al. (2015, 2016) compared the sexual activities that autistics and non-autistics conducted via the internet. Dewinter et al. (2016) compared six different sexual behaviours that autistics and non-autistics conducted online. They found that autistics used the internet more than non-autistics to talk about sex (40% vs. 38.3%), to show their genitalia or buttocks (10% vs. 6.7%), to arrange a sexual encounter (6.7% vs. 5%) and to watch pornography (83.3% vs 78.3%). In another study, Dewinter et al. (2015) stated that 54% of the autistic boys in their study used the internet for at least one sexually-related activity.

3.6   Sexual Behaviours

Dewinter et al. (2016) documented the sexual behaviours of autistic adolescents. The results in their study were based on the sexual experiences and behaviours of 30 autistic and 60 non-autistics. They discovered that autistics disclosed fewer instance of being in love (80% vs 95%), fewer experiences of dating (85% vs 66.7%), less sexual encounters with partners (91.57% vs 70%), and less kissing experiences (88.3% vs 70%). Dewinter et al. (2015) also documented the sexual experiences of autistic adolescents. They compared the sexual interests, behaviours and attitudes of 50 autistic adolescents (aged 15–18 years) of typical intelligence and 90 non-autistic adolescents of typical intelligence. Non-autistic adolescents reported more experiences of masturbation (81% vs 47%), dating (66% vs 35%), kissing (59% vs 28%), petting with clothes on (57% vs 26%), masturbating another (37% vs 20%), being masturbated (33% vs 17%), performing oral sex (23% vs 11%), receiving oral sex (29% vs 11%), and performing vaginal intercourse (30% vs 12%).

3.7 Conclusion

This chapter presented the main findings in the literature about the experiences and insights of autistics about their sexual behaviours, relationships, sexuality, and gender identity. It was revealed that autistics reported having a greater likelihood of identifying as either non-heterosexual or cisgender. Additionally, it was discovered that autistics do engage in online sexual activities, such as viewing sexually explicit material, meeting potential partners, or learning about contraception. Although the literature reviewed was diverse, many topics about sexuality and sexual behaviours were not identified. In the next chapter, these gaps in our knowledge are discussed along with justifications as to why these obscure research areas should be examined.

References

Barnett, J. P. (2017). Intersectional harassment and deviant embodiment among Autistic adults:(dis) ability, gender and sexuality. *Culture, Health & Sexuality, 19*(11), 1210–1224. https://doi.org/ 10.1080/13691058.2017.1309070

Barnett, J. P., & Maticka-Tyndale, E. (2015). Qualitative exploration of sexual experiences among adults on the autism spectrum: Implications for sex education. *Perspectives on Sexual and Reproductive Health, 47*(4), 171–179. https://doi.org/10.1363/47e5715

Brotto, L. A., & Yule, M. (2017). Asexuality: Sexual orientation, paraphilia, sexual dysfunction, or none of the above? *Archives of Sexual Behavior, 46*(3), 619–627. https://doi.org/10.1007/ s10508-016-0802-7

Brown-Lavoie, S. M., Viecili, M. A., & Weiss, J. A. (2014). Sexual knowledge and victimization in adults with autism spectrum disorders. *Journal of Autism and Developmental Disorders, 44*(9), 2185–2196. https://doi.org/10.1007/s10803-014-2093-y

Bush, H. H. (2019). Dimensions of sexuality among young women, with and without autism, with predominantly sexual minority identities. *Sexuality and Disability, 37*(2), 275–292. https://doi. org/10.1007/s11195-018-9532-1

Byers, E. S., & Nichols, S. (2014). Sexual satisfaction of high-functioning adults with autism spectrum disorder. *Sexuality and Disability, 32*(3), 365–382. https://doi.org/10.1007/s11195-014-9351-y

Byers, E. S., Nichols, S., & Voyer, S. D. (2013). Challenging stereotypes: Sexual functioning of single adults with high functioning autism spectrum disorder. *Journal of Autism and Developmental Disorders, 43*(11), 2617–2627. https://doi.org/10.1007/s10803-013-1813-z

Byers, E. S., Nichols, S., Voyer, S. D., & Reilly, G. (2013). Sexual well-being of a community sample of high-functioning adults on the autism spectrum who have been in a romantic relationship. *Autism, 17*(4), 418–433. https://doi.org/10.1177/1362361311431950

Cheak-Zamora, N. C., Teti, M., Maurer-Batjer, A., O'Connor, K. V., & Randolph, J. K. (2019). Sexual and relationship interest, knowledge, and experiences among adolescents and young adults with autism spectrum disorder. *Archives of Sexual Behavior, 48*(8), 2605–2615. https:// doi.org/10.1007/s10508-019-1445-2

Cooper, K., Smith, L. G., & Russell, A. J. (2018). Gender identity in autism: Sex differences in social affiliation with gender groups. *Journal of Autism and Developmental Disorders, 48*(12), 3995–4006. https://doi.org/10.1007/s10803-018-3590-1

De Vries, A. L., Noens, I. L., Cohen-Kettenis, P. T., van Berckelaer-Onnes, I. A., & Doreleijers, T. A. (2010). Autism spectrum disorders in gender dysphoric children and adolescents. *Journal of Autism and Developmental Disorders, 40*(8), 930–936. https://doi.org/10.1007/s10803-010-0935-9

Dewinter, J., De Graaf, H., & Begeer, S. (2017). Sexual orientation, gender identity, and romantic relationships in adolescents and adults with autism spectrum disorder. *Journal of Autism and Developmental Disorders, 47*(9), 2927–2934. https://doi.org/10.1007/s10803-017-3199-9

Dewinter, J., Van Parys, H., Vermeiren, R., & Van Nieuwenhuizen, C. (2017). Adolescent boys with an autism spectrum disorder and their experience of sexuality: An interpretative phenomenological analysis. *Autism, 21*(1), 75–82. https://doi.org/10.1177/1362361315627134

Dewinter, J., Vermeiren, R., Vanwesenbeeck, I., Lobbestael, J., & Van Nieuwenhuizen, C. (2015). Sexuality in adolescent boys with autism spectrum disorder: Self-reported behaviours and attitudes. *Journal of Autism and Developmental Disorders, 45*(3), 731–741. https://doi.org/10.1007/s10803-014-2226-3

Dewinter, J., Vermeiren, R. R. J. M., Vanwesenbeeck, I., & Van Nieuwenhuizen, C. (2016). Adolescent boys with autism spectrum disorder growing up: Follow-up of self-reported sexual experience. *European Child & Adolescent Psychiatry, 25*(9), 969–978. https://doi.org/10.1007/s00787-016-0816-7

Fernandes, L. C., Gillberg, C. I., Cederlund, M., Hagberg, B., Gillberg, C., & Billstedt, E. (2016). Aspects of sexuality in adolescents and adults diagnosed with autism spectrum disorders in childhood. *Journal of Autism and Developmental Disorders, 46*(9), 3155–3165. https://doi.org/10.1007/s10803-016-2855-9

Flanders, C. E., LeBreton, M. E., Robinson, M., Bian, J., & Caravaca-Morera, J. A. (2017). Defining bisexuality: Young bisexual and pansexual people's voices. *Journal of Bisexuality, 17*(1), 39–57. https://doi.org/10.1080/15299716.2016.1227016

George, R., & Stokes, M. A. (2018). A quantitative analysis of mental health among sexual and gender minority groups in ASD. *Journal of Autism and Developmental Disorders, 48*(6), 2052–2063. https://doi.org/10.1007/s10803-018-3469-1

Gilmour, L., Schalomon, P. M., & Smith, V. (2012). Sexuality in a community based sample of adults with autism spectrum disorder. *Research in Autism Spectrum Disorders, 6*(1), 313–318. https://doi.org/10.1016/j.rasd.2011.06.003

Hancock, G., Stokes, M. A., & Mesibov, G. (2019). Differences in romantic relationship experiences for individuals with an autism spectrum disorder. *Sexuality and Disability, 1*–15. https://doi.org/10.1007/s11195-019-09573-8

Hannah, L. A., & Stagg, S. D. (2016). Experiences of sex education and sexual awareness in young adults with autism spectrum disorder. *Journal of Autism and Developmental Disorders, 46*(12), 3678–3687. https://doi.org/10.1007/s10803-016-2906-2

Kanfiszer, L., Davies, F., & Collins, S. (2017). I was just so different: The experiences of women diagnosed with an autism spectrum disorder in adulthood in relation to gender and socialrelationships. *Autism, 21*(6), 661–669. https://doi.org/10.1177/1362361316687987

Losty, M., & O'Connor, J. (2018). Falling outside of the 'nice little binary box': A psychoanalytic exploration of the non-binary gender identity. *Psychoanalytic Psychotherapy, 32*(1), 40–60. https://doi.org/10.1080/02668734.2017.1384933

May, T., Pang, K. C., & Williams, K. (2017). Brief report: Sexual attraction and relationships in adolescents with autism. *Journal of Autism and Developmental Disorders, 47*(6), 1910–1916. https://doi.org/10.1007/s10803-017-3092-6

Mehzabin, P., & Stokes, M. A. (2011). Self-assessed sexuality in young adults with high-functioning autism. *Research in Autism Spectrum Disorders, 5*(1), 614–621. https://doi.org/10.1016/j.rasd.2010.07.006

Mogavero, M. C., & Hsu, K. H. (2019). Dating and courtship behaviors among those with autism spectrum disorder. *Sexuality and Disability, 1*–10. https://doi.org/10.1007/s11195-019-09565-8

Mundle, G., Mahler, L., & Bhugra, D. (2015). Homosexuality and mental health. *International Review of Psychiatry, 27*(5), 355–356. https://doi.org/10.3109/09540261.2015.1109790

Pearlman-Avnion, S., Cohen, N., & Eldan, A. (2017). Sexual well-being and quality of life among high-functioning adults with autism. *Sexuality and Disability, 35*(3), 279–293. https://doi.org/10.1007/s11195-017-9490-z

Rosenthal, A. M., Sylva, D., Safron, A., & Bailey, J. M. (2011). Sexual arousal patterns of bisexual men revisited. *Biological Psychology, 88*(1), 112–115. https://doi.org/10.1016/j.biopsycho.2011.06.015

Roth, M. E., & Gillis, J. M. (2015). "Convenience with the click of a mouse": A survey of adults with autism spectrum disorder on online dating. *Sexuality and Disability, 33*(1), 133–150. https://doi.org/10.1007/s11195-014-9392-2

Roughgarden, J. (2017). Homosexuality and evolution: A critical appraisal. In *On human nature* (pp. 495–516). Academic Press.

Savin-Williams, R. C., & Cohen, K. M. (2018). Prevalence, mental health, and heterogeneity of bisexual men. *Current Sexual Health Reports, 10*(3), 196–202. https://doi.org/10.1007/s11930-018-0164-3

Stotzer, R. L., Ka'opua, L. S. I., & Diaz, T. P. (2014). Is healthcare caring in Hawaii? Preliminary results from a health assessment of Lesbian, Gay, Bisexual, Transgender, Questioning, and Intersex people in four counties. *Hawai'i Journal of Medicine & Public Health, 73*(6), 175.

Strang, J. F., Powers, M. D., Knauss, M., Sibarium, E., Leibowitz, S. F., Kenworthy, L., et al. (2018). "They thought it was an obsession": Trajectories and perspectives of autistic transgender and gender-diverse adolescents. *Journal of Autism and Developmental Disorders, 48*(12), 4039–4055. https://doi.org/10.1007/s10803-018-3723-6

Strunz, S., Schermuck, C., Ballerstein, S., Ahlers, C. J., Dziobek, I., & Roepke, S. (2017). Romantic relationships and relationship satisfaction among adults with Asperger syndrome and high-functioning autism. *Journal of Clinical Psychology, 73*(1), 113–125. https://doi.org/10.1002/jclp.22319

van der Miesen, A. I., Hurley, H., Bal, A. M., & de Vries, A. L. (2018). Prevalence of the wish to be of the opposite gender in adolescents and adults with autism spectrum disorder. *Archives of Sexual Behavior, 47*(8), 2307–2317. https://doi.org/10.1007/s10508-018-1218-3

Chapter 4
Recommendations for Research in the Future and Final Comments

4.1 Contraception

The studies examined in this scoping review did not contain any references to autistic adults describing their experiences and insights about contraception, which can be a fundamental aspect of some sexual relationships, where pregnancy is possible but not desired. It is possible that the approach used to retrieve examined studies, such as the key terms used or the databases searched, could have inhibited the location of such research. To ensure that the research methodology was not the cause of this lack of literature being examined a general search of Google Scholar was conducted with the key words *'contraception'* and *'autism'* or *'autistic'*. This search showed that there are studies that have explored if contraceptive usage contributes to the development of autism (Strifert, 2014) as well as studies about educating autistic girls on how to use contraception (Tullis & Zangrillo, 2013). Although these studies are a welcome addition, the lack of literature published about this topic does present a series of opportunities for possible research in the future.

Since there is a paucity of literature about autistic adults' experiences of choosing and using contraception there are many areas where additional research can be conducted in the future about this topic. Women have a variety of contraceptive options, such as contraceptive pills, Intra Uterine Devices, and vaginal rings. In the future, it would be advantageous to study which contraceptive options autistic women find the most suitable and why. It might be that sensory sensitivities might prevent autistic women from asking male partners to use condoms, or from using vaginal rings, leaving the contraceptive pill or an Intra Uterine Device as the most suitable options. However, it might be that there are higher rates of complications or failure of the contraceptive pill for autistic women, who may have one or more co-occurring conditions or executive functioning issues that make it difficult to remember to take the pill every day. Another potential avenue for research in the future is learning how autistic women have broached the subject with their sexual

M. Bennett, E. Goodall, *Sexual Behaviours and Relationships of Autistics*,
SpringerBriefs in Well-Being and Quality of Life Research,
https://doi.org/10.1007/978-3-030-65599-0_4

partners about wanting to use contraception, and if they would have liked to learn about ways to discuss this during sex education at school.

Unlike females, males do not have many contraceptive options. Currently, condoms and vasectomies are their only contraceptive options, with the latter not protecting against all sexually transmitted diseases. There is a lack of research about autistic males and their experiences or views about and insights into contraception. This lack of research has had an impact on the ability of parents to discuss such topics with their autistic sons (Nichols & Blakeley-Smith, 2009). It is important that research be conducted in this area so that parents and teachers feel confident and comfortable discussing contraception with autistic males. To achieve this outcome, it would be prudent to ask autistic males about their knowledge of contraception, such as how to use a condom. Determining their level of knowledge can help future generations of educators and parents develop a better understanding about how to educate autistic males about their contraceptive options, which can have flow on effects in terms of reducing instances of unplanned parenthood and reducing the proliferation of sexually transmitted infections. The effectiveness of condoms is reliant upon their being used properly, which may or may not be understood by individual autistics. The use of condoms also requires preplanning, good hand-eye co-ordination and an understanding of, and ability to place the condom correctly on the penis, and remove it without spilling any semen. Many of these steps may be more problematic for autistics, especially if they have been unable to access and correctly interpret explicit and literal explanations of these steps.

Research around the use of contraception by autistics could examine both barriers to effective use of contraceptives and the supports that overcome those barriers. For example, if a large percentage of autistics are allergic to latex, they could use non-latex condoms. If people find it hard to remember when to take a daily pill they could use timers on their phones, or longer acting implants. The effectiveness of contraceptive education for autistic young people and adults would also be a useful avenue of research.

For many years, researchers have attempted to develop more contraceptive options for men. One such avenue of research and development has been a contraceptive pill. Although different drugs have been researched as potential candidates, they have not been found to be effective for mainstream usage (Roth, Page, & Bremner, 2016; Wang, Festin, & Swerdloff, 2016). Despite there being no oral contraceptive medications available for males, this has not prevented their views about such medication from being examined (Wilson, 2018). Before the introduction of this medication into mainstream clinical use, research about the views of autistic males about oral contraception should be conducted. Such research might uncover the view that they prefer an oral contraceptive, especially if they have sensory sensitivities to the feel and/or smell of condoms. However, the benefits and drawbacks of oral contraceptives versus condoms for autistic males remains theoretical since there is no research about this topic.

4.2 Lesbian, Gay, Bisexual, Transgender, Intersex and Asexual (LGBTQIA+)

4.2.1 Coming Out

The act of revealing one's non-heterosexual sexual orientation or non cis-gender identification is colloquially referred to as *'coming out'*. Some individuals come out to only a few people while others are more public in proclaiming their sexual orientation; for example, broadcasting this information in the form of a YouTube video to a global audience (Craig & McInroy, 2014; Wuest, 2014). A diverse variety of people in society have come out, including famous sports stars (Brennan, 2018; Cleland, Magrath, & Kian, 2018), corporate workers (Fielden & Jepson, 2016), prisoners (Maschi, Rees, & Klein, 2016), and celebrities (Lovelock, 2017). In contrast, there is a scarcity of literature about LGBTQIA+ autistics describing their coming out experiences (Bennett & Goodall, 2016).

The act of deliberately coming out often requires someone anticipating how others might respond to this revelation, as it can still be a risky action. Some studies have suggested that autistics often lack the ability to conceptualise another's views and perspectives proficiently (Livingston et al., 2019; Schuwerk, Vuori, & Sodian, 2015). Due to difficulties with social communication, there is an increased probability that autistics would come out at inappropriate times or to people who will react with hostility towards such a revelation. In order to reduce the likelihood of this social rejection occurring it is important that research be conducted into discovering strategies that can help autistics decide when, where, and how to safely come out to others. It may be that many non-heterosexual or non-cis-gendered autistics do not ever come out, and this would be an interesting area of research to ascertain how and why individual autistics maintain their gender and/or sexual orientation identities without publicly declaring them.

4.2.2 Homophobia

With increased rates of non-heterosexuality in the autistic population, they may be at increased risk of homophobia. Sears and Williams (1997, p. 15) have defined homophobia as an *"overt violence, such as physical assault and verbal harassment, to psychological battering resulting in fear of self-disclosure or the absence of same-gender intimacy, to social and political offensives … that have fostered and reinforced anti-gay sentiments and behaviors'*. Homophobia can occur in many settings, including the workplace (Howell, 2018), family environment (Wakefield, Kalinauskaite, & Hopkins, 2016), or at school (Dentato et al., 2016). A review of the literature showed that there is a lack of research about homosexual and bisexual autistics describing their experiences of homophobia. This point was expressed by Bennett and Goodall (2016), who argued that more research should be conducted into the experiences of homophobia by LGBTQIA+ autistics. Conducting research about this topic can produce many benefits for autistics, especially considering that the proportion of homosexuality is greater within the autistic population than the non-autistic population (Cooper, Smith, & Russell, 2018; Dewinter, De Graff, & Begeer, 2017; Mogavero & Hsu, 2019). Homophobia has been identified as a cause of depression and mental health issues for homosexual and bisexual people (Dentato et al., 2016). It is logical to assume that the homophobic encounters that LGBTQIA+ autistics experience can also produce the same outcomes. By understanding how non-heterosexual autistics experience homophobia, strategies can be developed which can help improve their mental health.

Research in this area may firstly need to focus on what autistics understand and interpret as homophobia, as it may be difficult for individuals who may have been bullied to discriminate between bullying behaviour and specifically homophobic behaviours. Humphrey and Hebron (2015) review found that although research estimates varied, the bullying of autistics in school was consistently high, with up to 95% of autistic students reporting bullying. It is unknown how much of this was due to emerging sexuality or gender expression and how much was targeting the individuals characteristics of autism.

4.2.3 Transphobia

In this scoping review four studies documented the proportion of their sample of autistics who identified as transgender (Barnett, 2017; Cooper, Smith, & Russell, 2018; George & Stokes, 2018; Mogavero & Hsu, 2019). With the exception of Barnett (2017), who did not compare the proportion of transgender individuals within an autistic sample to a control group, the other three studies about this topic reported that the proportion of transgender individuals within the autistic sample was greater than in the non-autistic sample. Although these studies are a welcome addition to this small amount of research, they fail to address research questions about the life experiences of transgender autistics (Bennett & Goodall, 2016), such as transphobia and other forms of transgender-specific forms of discrimination (e.g., discrimination in employment) and more positive experiences related to being able to express who themselves authentically.

Transphobia, a form of discrimination against transgender people, has been identified as a factor contributing to the high rates of suicidality within the transgender community. Rates of suicidality within this community have been estimated to be over 30% (Clements-Nolle, Marx, & Katz, 2006). Some non-autistic transgender people have described the coping strategies which they have used to avoid committing suicide, such as seeking support from loved ones or through being aware and vigilant against mental states that they regard as adversely affecting their mental health (Hunt, Morrow, & McGuire, 2019; Mizock et al., 2017). For transgender autistics, however, the coping strategies that they have used to mitigate suicide have not been researched in detail. It could be that due to difficulties within social situations, they do not have a network of family and friends that they can use to access support and protect them from committing suicide. Additionally, transgender autistics might have atypical interoception, and so not have developed a sense of awareness of the build-up of negative emotional states. This can lead to feeling extremely distressed without having noticed the build-up of distress when it would have been more manageable. It is possible that this can contribute to them taking their own life. By comparing the transphobia experiences of autistic and non-autistic transgender people it might be possible to discover the techniques that people in both groups have used to protect themselves from transphobic incidents. Such information might help transgender autistics who have not yet acquired the necessary life experience and skills that they can use to protect themselves as they encounter incidents of transphobia.

In addition, it would be useful to further research the unique issues faced by autistics seeking input from health professionals to further their gender transition. Strang et al. (2018) reported that gender diverse autistics faced additional barriers from health professionals because of their autism diagnosis, with accusations of simply being 'obsessed' with gender non-conformity or transition. Research into this area would complement the small study by Strang et al.'s 2018 study which looked at trajectories and perspectives of twenty two autistic transgender and gender-diverse adolescents.

Another area of research need in the area if transgender autistics is whether they face barriers to autism assessment and diagnosis prior to their transition that do not exist post transition. Anecdotally, transgender autistic adults have reported that their autism presented in a way that was more typical of their gender and not their birth gender. Although there is widespread disagreement amongst researchers whether or not autism contains gendered phenotypes. Strang et al. (2020) suggest that all autism research and clinical practice should take into account sex-and gender-related factors.

4.2.4   Gender Reassignment Surgery (GRS)

Gender reassignment surgery (GRS) is a medical procedure in which a transgender person changes their physical appearance so that it matches the gender identity that they identify as being. GRS is often an extremely personal, private, and life-changing experience (Selvaggi & Bellringer, 2011). GRS has been found to improve the quality of life of transgender people who have transitioned from a male-to-female outward gender identity (Ainsworth & Spiegel, 2010). GRS has also been a subject of films; for example, Transamerica (Jensen, 2018). Despite there being a small amount of literature about GRS, there still remains a lack of literature about transgender autistics and their life experiences of GRS. The need to study this topic is important considering that many studies have shown that a greater proportion of the autistic population identified as transgender than those in the non-autistic population (Cooper et al., 2018; George & Stokes, 2018; Mogavero & Hsu, 2019).

Aside from obtaining extra knowledge, which will further our understanding of the autism spectrum, insights from transgender autistics about their GRS experiences will undoubtedly equip future generations of transgender autistics with important knowledge that they can use as they embark on their gender reassignment journey.

Research could also be conducted into the rationale provided by autistics for both choosing to undertake GRS and not to, as well as the life satisfaction outcomes in both cases. It may be that this research could identify significant mental health protective factors for transgender autistics.

4.2.5   Asexuality

Asexuality is generally considered a sexual orientation, like heterosexuality, homosexuality, and bisexuality. In his scoping review, six studies reported the proportion of autistics within their sample who identified as asexual (Barnett & Maticka-Tyndale, 2015; Barnett, 2017; Bush, 2019; Dewinter, De Graaf, & Begeer, 2017; May, Pang, & Williams, 2017; Roth & Gillis, 2015). These studies showed that this proportion was greater than for non-autistics. For instance, May et al. (2017) showed that autistic males were more inclined to be asexual than their non-autistic counterparts, 9% and 3% respectfully. Similarly, Dewinter, De Graaf, and Begeer (2017) reported greater proportions of asexuality in their sample of autistic males than in their sample of non-autistic males (4.7% and 1.1% respectfully) and in their sample of autistic females than in their sample of non-autistic females (14.9% and 1.6% respectfully).

Although asexuality is more prevalent in the autistic population than in the non-autistic population there still remains scant research about the experiences of asexual autistics (Bennett & Goodall, 2016). In the future research could be conducted into exploring the potential conflict that arises when asexual autistics are negotiating with their partners what intimate activities, they feel comfortable participating in as this has been described as an issue by Goodall (2016). Another area of research that could be explored is how asexual autistics construct and portray their asexual identity to their friends. In other words, *'how do autistics come to conclude that they are asexual and what do asexual autistics say to their friends about their sexual orientation?'* This research has the potential to help future generations of asexual autistics as they develop their understanding of their sexual orientation. It may be that many more autistics are asexual, but do not know what asexuality is and are mistaking a lack of sexual desire for sensory dislike for sexual intimacy, as discussed by Goodall (2016). This could be very simply rectified by including asexuality in sex education in schools, should research find a significant lack of knowledge of asexuality in autistics and/or the general population.

4.3 Pregnancy and Childbirth

Pregnancy and childbirth are one of the possible outcomes of some sexual relationships and activities. Without adequate information about this, it is possible that autistics may experience higher rates of unplanned pregnancies. An analysis of the studies collected for this scoping review showed that no studies have been published about the pregnancy and childbirth experiences of autistic women. There are three plausible reasons for why this topic has not been examined in detail. First, Bennett, Webster, Goodall, and Rowland (2018) have proposed that there is a prevailing attitude within society towards infantilizing autistics. Due to this attitude, many have concluded that autistics are not interested in sex and, by extension, are also not interested in having children. Second, according to Jang et al. (2014), there is a tendency to focus on conducting research into autistic children instead of autistic adults. This focus has meant that the sexual behaviours of autistic adults, including the pregnancy and childbirth experiences of autistic women, have not been explored. Third, several researchers have proposed that autistic women and girls can camouflage their autistic characteristics which makes it difficult for them to be diagnosed and targeted for research (Dean, Harwood, & Kasari, 2017; Gould, 2017). However, with more research being conducted on autistic females this trend is reversing.

A search through the broader literature about the autism spectrum revealed two studies about autistic women and their pregnancy and birthing experiences (Gardner, Suplee, Bloch, & Lecks, 2016; Rogers, Lepherd, Ganguly, & Jacob-Rogers, 2017). Gardner et al. (2016) published a qualitative study in which they described the childbearing experiences of eight women who had a diagnosis of Asperger syndrome. Based on the experiences reported they recommended that midwives and clinicians provide supports that are tailored to the autistic patient's needs and which take into consideration the specific sensory experiences of women with Asperger syndrome. Additionally, they recommend that healthcare professionals counsel such women about strategies that they can use to cope with sensory intrusions as well as adjusting the clinical environment to decrease sensory stimuli that they may find distressing and overwhelming. Rogers et al. (2017) also reported that autistic women encountered sensory difficulties during their birthing experiences.

For more research to be conducted into the pregnancy and birthing experiences of autistic women there needs to be two changes to how we approach studying the autism spectrum. First, the myth that autistic women and gender diverse autistics with ovaries and a uterus, are not interested in sex or becoming mothers needs to be dispelled (Bennett et al., 2018). By dispelling this myth, it is possible that autistics will not be infantilised. Second, more research needs to be conducted into refining the diagnostic criteria so that it is more sensitive to detecting the subtle autistic features that autistic women and girls display. By perfecting such diagnostic systems more autistic women and girls can receive appropriate supports and there would be a greater pool of potential autistic female candidates for autism research.

It would be helpful if the experience of pregnancy for autistics was further researched, to ascertain if pregnancy impacts the sensory and communication challenges usually experienced by that individual and if there are any impacts, if these remain post-partum or not.

Hollocks, Lerh, Magiati, Meiser-Stedman, and Brugha's (2019) systematic review and meta-analysis of anxiety and depression in autistic adults confirmed that these adults experience much higher rates of 'current' and lifetime anxiety and depression. However, there was no research looking at post-partum or post-natal depression in autistic mothers. It is unknown at this point if autistics experience this time of depression more than non-autistic mothers. The difficulty of diagnostic clarity and atypical presentations of depression may make it harder for autistic mothers to be diagnosed and receive support, or it may be that they themselves and their partners, if they have a partner, are unaware of the depression and so do not seek support.

Further research on the experiences of autistics accessing health supports both for pregnancy and post-partum, would be useful to ensure that expectant autistic parents are supported effectively by health professionals, going forward. For example, effective supports are more likely to pick up post-partum and post-natal depression and implement treatment and practical support strategies earlier that if the autistic parents are not effectively being engaged with.

4.4   Parenting

Many autistic adults raise children, whether they are their biological children or not. Parenting can be the logical outcome of some relationships, where blended families are formed, and it is unknown how autistic adults adjust to this role of parenting within a blended family. There is a considerable amount of research about parents raising autistic children. Most of this research has focused on the experiences of mothers (Bonis, 2016; Rankin, Paisley, Tomeny, & Eldred, 2019; Sim, Cordier, Vaz, & Falkmer, 2019). However, there are a few studies about the experiences of fathers raising autistic children (Cheuk & Lashewicz, 2016; Meadan, Stoner, & Angell, 2015; O'Halloran, Sweeney, & Doody, 2013). In contrast, there is a very small amount of research about autistic parents. The reasons why there has been a lack of research on this topic has never been clearly explained. However, it is possible that not much research has been conducted into this topic because it is commonly believed that autistics are not capable of being parents arising out of the myth that they are not interested in having sexual relationships (Bennett et al., 2018).

There are many areas where research can be conducted into the experiences of autistic parents. First, researchers could examine how such parents navigate parenting whilst maintaining the adult relationship. Second, researchers could examine how such parents bring up their children, in particular how they observe, comprehend and respond to undesirable behaviour. Third, researchers could explore how such parents coordinate their family responsibilities with their work commitments. Additionally, it would be very interesting to research if autistic parents, parent autistic and non-autistic offspring differently to the ways non-autistic parents, parent their autistic and non-autistic offspring and if there are any significant differential outcomes. Goodall (2016) presented a number of quotes from autistic parents that illustrated some of the ways sensory challenges impacted some aspects of parenting, and in contrast how some autistic parents enjoyed sharing interests with their child for both educational purposes and for fun. By examining these issues, our understanding of autism in adulthood will increase and the focus will shift from predominantly researching autistic children to exploring some of the parenting skills and challenges faced by autistic adults.

In contrast to this, it is unknown how many adult autistics do not want to become parents and chose not to procreate or give birth to their own children. Research in this area could look at why autistics do or do not want to become parents and how they communicate this to potential and current partners. Parenting through a blended family is complex for anyone, research could help to identify what supports autistics feel would support them to parent effectively in a blended family.

4.5   Domestic/Family Violence

It is known that women with disabilities are disproportionately victims of sexual violence and domestic/family violence (Ballan & Freyer, 2012). The amount of research about domestic/family violence that non-autistics experience is extremely large. In contrast, during the literature search phase of this scoping review no studies were identified which described the domestic violence experiences of autistics. Griffiths et al. (2019) reported that autistics are more likely to have been victims of domestic/family violence, as well as more likely to be victims of sexual violence that non-autistics. In the future, research into this topic should be conducted for several reasons. First, domestic violence can sometimes be subtle and not obvious. For example, it can present itself in the form of insistent questioning and invasions of privacy, or financial abuse. For some autistics, they might not have the social communication skills to detect or seek help in relation to such subtle forms of abuse. By conducting research, it might be possible to learn about how best to support autistics who are in relationships with subtle forms of domestic violence. Second, sometimes people are unaware of how to escape situations of domestic violence, regardless of whether they are autistic or not. Researching the best ways to support autistics to safely leave situations involving domestic violence will help people in these circumstances escape such situations.

Griffiths et al. (2019) also reported that autistics experience higher rates of bullying and victimisation in childhood, which may contribute to a lack of awareness and understanding of the difference between healthy and unhealthy/toxic/dangerous relationships. It would be useful to research whether autistic teens and adults can easily identify behaviours that indicate a relationship is or is not healthy and safe to remain in. If not research on how best to convey these concepts to autistics effectively would be helpful. Goodall's (2016) book for autistics presented clear information on this topic in response to autistic community feedback.

4.6   Relationship Breakup and Divorce

In many different countries, such as the United Kingdom and Australia, some couples end their marital relationship with a divorce (Skew, Evans, & Gray, 2009). It is unknown if autistics divorce or end long term relationships at greater or lesser rates than non-autistics. There is a lot of literature about the personal ramifications that non-autistics experience when they have a relationship breakup or divorce (Couch, Tamborini, & Reznik, 2015; De Vaus, Gray, Qu, & Stanton, 2017; Fisher & Low, 2015; McKeever & Wolfinger, 2001; Tach & Eads, 2015; Tamborini, Couch, & Reznik, 2015). In contrast, a review of the available literature did not show any studies about this topic for autistic adults. It is possible that research into the relationship breakup and divorce experiences of autistic adults is important, especially considering that they might have a greater need for supports since they generally have a small number of people who they know who can support them once they exit a relationship or marriage. Additionally, divorce and relationship breakups can provoke a wide range of emotional responses, such as sadness and anger. Dealing with these emotional issues might be difficult for some autistics and consequently warrant additional investigation.

Goodall (2016) reviewed reasons why autistics may want to end relationships, providing a range of scenarios, including unhealthy or abusive relationships. A couple of examples provided, indicated that some autistics may be less resilient during a divorce or other legally mediated break-up and so end up with virtually nothing even if they are legally entitled to more. This is an area that would benefit from research, as if autistic adults do not understand their rights and responsibilities during divorce or other legally mediated break-ups, they may disproportionately lose out during this process. It is also possible that social communication difficulties, which are at the core of an autism spectrum diagnosis, impact the ability of autistic adults to effectively participate in legal negotiations, including custody issues and asset distribution.

Other anecdotes presented (Goodall, 2016), suggest that for some autistic adults, awareness of how unhealthy their relationship is, comes only from friends or family members. A number of the autistic adults mention not realising breaking up/leaving was an option, or not understanding until after their spouse/partner left them, that life was better without the relationship that it was with it. Research into how autistic adults understand and navigate healthy versus unhealthy relationships would enable counsellors and psychologists to tailor support for their autistic clients in the area of relationships. Specifically, research on the vulnerability of autistics to manipulative or abusive relationships would be useful. It would be of great help to autistics to understand the 'red flags' of manipulative or abusive relationships and how/when to seek help safely.

4.7   Sex Education

During the literature search phase of the scoping review process eight studies were retrieved which explored the benefits and drawbacks of autistics participating in sex education programs (Corona, Fox, Christodulu, & Worlock, 2016; Dekker et al., 2015; Holmes & Himle, 2014; Holmes, Strassberg, & Himle, 2019; Mackin, Loew, Gonzalez, Tykol, & Christensen, 2016; Nichols & Blakeley-Smith, 2009; Pryde & Jahoda, 2018; Visser et al., 2015). An inspection of these studies showed that parents of autistic children were interviewed, but not autistics and thus the research did not meet the eligibility criteria. Such studies were excluded because the views and insights of parents might have distorted the views of autistics, especially if parents and their autistic offspring discussed the research study before or during their participation in the study. Since these studies were excluded there was no research identified that has exclusively explored autistics and their experiences of sex education programs. Despite this lack of research, there is a need for more research into this topic to be conducted; especially considering that traditional sex education programs might not offer autistics a sufficient amount of understanding about the complicated and nuanced nature of intimate and relationships.

There are a few sex and relationship education resources specifically for autistics adults, created by or with autistic adults, including an interactive website from Organisation for Autism Research (OAR) (2019); Sex Ed for Self-Advocates, and a book from Goodall (2016); *The autism spectrum guide to sexuality and relationships: Understand yourself and make choices that are right for you*. These contain very clear messages using logical and literal language in two different formats. Marks (2020), suggests that there is a clear need for sex and relationship education for autistic adults, based on her work as an educator for children and adults with intellectual disabilities and/or and autism spectrum diagnosis, stating that her clients "need safe places to ask honest questions about all of these aspects — without shame." The aspects included are communication, sex and relationships from start to finish. It would be useful to formally evaluate if resources designed with/by autistics provide more or less effective sex and relationship education for autistics, than resources for the general public and why. There may be an assumption that adults do not need sex and relationship education or support, however, the anecdotes provided from adult autistics within both the OAR (2019) and Goodall (2016) resources, suggest otherwise.

Another aspect of sex education is awareness and understanding of sexual health and sexually transmitted diseases and infections. It is currently unknown whether safe sex messages are understood and effectively implemented by autistic adults, nor whether they are more or less at risk of sexual health difficulties and/or diseases. Research in this area would enable public health campaigns to be as effective as possible for this cohort, whilst ensuring health practitioners were equipped to communicate using evidence informed ways.

4.8   Engaging People on the Autism Spectrum as Research Participants

The reader can infer from the topics mentioned above that there remain some areas where research in the future can be conducted. However, it is equally important to use research practices that are comfortable for most people on the autism spectrum. To this end, this section will outline several practical strategies that researchers could use when they are conducting inclusive research with people on the autism spectrum about topics that they might find sensitive and/or confronting (Cascio et al., 2020; Fletcher-Watson et al., 2019). The strategies explained below relate to the conduct that researchers should perform with participants on the autism spectrum through the entire research process with using either an in-depth interview or focus group method for data collection.

4.8.1   Conducting a Pilot Study

Before a researcher conducts a study in which potential participants on the autism spectrum are expected to recall in detail their experiences and views of sensitive issues, such as sexual relationships, it would be advantageous for the researcher to conduct a pilot study. A pilot study has the potential for a researcher to identify and remedy any logistical and administrative barriers that prevent people on the autism spectrum from participating in the study. For example, while conducting a pilot study a researcher might discover that some participants on the autism spectrum have difficulties interpreting the questions asked to them or that they might have difficulty finding the room where the interview or focus group session will occur. Once such issues have been discovered a researcher could remedy these issues by rephrasing the questions posed to the participants or placing signage around the building to help the participant find the room where the interview or focus group session will occur (Cooperative Research Centre for Living with Autism Spectrum Disorders (AutismCRC), 2014).

4.8.2   Testing Interview or Focus Group Session Questions

It has been acknowledged in the literature about the autism spectrum, as well as in conventional diagnostic instruments (e.g., *Diagnostic and Statistical Manual of Mental Disorders - Fifth edition*), that some people on the autism spectrum interpret verbal and/or writing literally (American Psychiatric Association (APA), 2013). Such literal interpretations can be problematic for some on the autism spectrum. For example, if an interview question contains words that are ambiguous, or have multiple meanings, a participant could misinterpret the question and then provide an answer that the participant believes answers the question but from the interviewer's perspective appears to be verbose and evasive. In turn, the interviewer could probe for additional information which might appear to some on the autism spectrum as a sign that the interviewer does not trust them. Such impressions can hinder what is supposed to be a comfortable and uneventful collection of information. To avoid this potential outcome, it is prudent for a researcher to conduct a pilot study with a small sample of people on the autism spectrum to evaluate if they understand the potential interview questions. Such a pilot study can potentially identify questions that might be ambiguous and which, in turn, might need to be rephrased (AutismCRC, 2014).

4.8.3 Adjusting the Consent Process

In many countries, such as Australia, it is an ethical and legal requirement that participants must provide written consent, usually via a signed consent form, before participating in a study. Consent is often granted after they have been comprehensively informed about the nature of the study. Additionally, a participant's consent is also obtained after the researcher has explained to them the possible outcomes of their expected involvement, such as the potential risks associated with their participation. In the event that the participant is not able to provide written consent, either because they are a minor or have been deemed to be mentally incapacitated to make an informed decision, then a legal representative can consent on their behalf (National Health and Medical Research Council (NHMRC), 2018).

Obtaining consent from participants is not a simple administrative task. Before a participant grants consent, a comprehensive induction should occur between the potential participant and the researcher. This induction should explain many elements of the research process, including:

- the potential risks that the participant may encounter in the study and appropriate mitigation strategies;
- the steps and processes that will be used once the interview or focus group session ends that maintains the participant's anonymity;
- a reassurance that participation in the study is voluntary and that if the participant decides to terminate their involvement whilst in the study that their information will be destroyed and that there will be no negative legal, financial, or personal repercussions for their decision;
- whether participants will be able to obtain a copy of their interview transcript/ other contributions so that they can confirm if their views were accurately recorded;
- whether participants will be able to access a copy of the study prior to its publication to confirm that their insights and experiences have not been taken out of context;
- under what circumstances would the researcher be legally obligated to inform the authorities of potential crimes. For example, during an interview session if an

adult participant reveals that they have molested a child then the researcher may need to inform the authorities of this self-confessed crime;

- how the researcher will store all the data collected. For example, all interview transcripts will be password protected or all hard copy transcripts will be stored in a locked filing cabinet;
- who in the research team will have access to the data that the participant provides. For example, if the research is part of a PhD study will their supervisors also have access to the data provided by the participants;
- a list of support services that participants can contact after participating in the study if they feel that the topics that they have discussed are emotionally difficult and confronting; and
- discussing with the participants if they would like their contributions once de-identified to be made accessible to other researchers (AutismCRC, 2014; NHMRC, 2018).

For some on the autism spectrum they will require additional guidance and support from the researcher as they are inducted through the consent process. A researcher might wish to implement the following steps since it is incumbent upon them to ensure that the participant fully understands both the nature of the project and the potential consequences that they might encounter during and after their participation. The researcher should:

- ensure that any information that is written on the information sheet for the participants and/or the consent form is clear, concise, and comprehensive;
- give potential participants the opportunity to ask any questions that they might have about their involvement in the study; and
- be clear about what the participant will be required to do during the study and ensure that the steps explained are identical to the steps that are listed on any handouts (AutismCRC, 2014; NHMRC, 2018).

4.8.4 Orientation Before the Interview or Focus Group Sessions

Some people on the autism spectrum find the task of leaving their familiar surroundings, like their home, and participating in a study that is conducted in an unfamiliar environment daunting and stressful. It can also be challenging if they have to disrupt their daily routines to attend the appointment. To mitigate this potential confusion and stress, before participating in a study the researcher might want to consider using the following strategies:

- meet with the potential participant on the autism spectrum in-person before inducting them through the consent process. This encounter would give the potential participant the opportunity to get to know the researcher as a person;

- consider the participant's scheduled to avoid situations where they might have to navigate peak traffic times or busy times at places of research. For example, if the study is being conducted at a university campus it might be advantageous to not schedule an appointment when there is a class change where lifts and corridors would be crowded with students;
- prior to the interview session occurring to help the potential participants find the place where the interview or focus group session will occur the researcher may want to give them a handout that has pictures of the building, the door where they would need to use to enter the building, and any key landmarks near the building. To augment this handout the researcher may want to place signs at the building's entry points, lifts, and in corridors to help steer the potential participant to the room where the study will be conducted;
- to help the potential participants arrive at the institution where the interview will be conducted the researcher may want to provide a parking voucher or a stipend to reimburse them for the costs that they have paid for transport;
- provide the potential participant with a mobile/cell phone number that they can call or text if they need the researcher's help; and
- the researcher might want to send a text message to the potential participant to remind them on the day when and where the interview or focus group session is scheduled to occur. For some on the autism spectrum they might prefer receiving text messages since they can respond to such messages when they are ready as opposed to answering a telephone call when they are not prepared. Additionally, a text message will have the information documented which is easier for some on the autism spectrum since they will not need to remember the meeting details discussed during a telephone call (AutismCRC, 2014; NHMRC, 2018).

4.8.5   Creating a Comfortable Environment for Participants on the Autism Spectrum

Some people on the autism spectrum have sensory sensitivities to environmental stimuli (Kuiper, Verhoeven, & Geurts, 2019; Muratori et al., 2017; Wicker, Monfardini, & Royet, 2016). Such sensitivities can interfere with their ability to provide both informed consent and comprehensive answers to research questions. Thus, before they provide their informed consent to participate in a study the researchers should modify the environment where the data collection is to occur so that both they and the participant can feel comfortable. As listed in Table 4.1, the AutismCRC has provided the following strategies to modify the physical environment to make it more sensorially comfortable for participants on the autism spectrum.

Table 4.1 Creating autistic-friendly environments for research

Factor	Recommendation
Structuring the Physical Environment	Ensuring that environments are clear from clutter and organized with everything in its place can support individuals with ASD. This can also decrease anxiety levels by creating predictability. Individuals with ASD may also have difficulty processing sensory information. By understanding their sensory needs and making small changes to the physical environment, sensory sensitivities can be addressed to increase engagement and participation. Whether you are interviewing, observing or engaging an individual with ASD in assessment tasks, there are some important considerations in making the environment ASD friendly.
Distractions	• Ensure the environment is quiet and there is minimal background noise (even the sound of a ticking clock on the wall can be distracting for some individuals). • Consider the temperature of the environment and check that with the person. • Avoid rooms with ceiling fans in summer as these can be very distracting for some individuals with ASD. • Avoid venetian blinds that go down to the floor as these can be distracting for young children. • Avoid too many pictures/posters on walls and too much visual clutter. Just have the necessary objects that you need for the research activities in the room. • Individuals with ASD benefit from working in an environment which has clearly defined areas and boundaries for specific tasks. Children often perform better when facing a wall or in a cubicle/carrel. • Ensure correct size and style of furniture (chairs, tables, desk etc.) for the individual's age and dimensions (e.g., child's feet on the floor at low table and chair)
Lighting	Some individuals with ASD are hypersensitive to bright lights or fluorescent lights. This may adversely affect their concentration, interaction and behaviour. • Use as much natural light as possible or alternatively try to use lower levels of light. • Consider the type of lighting—fluorescent lights can be too bright. Ensure there are no flickering lights/bulbs. • It is often not the lights themselves but the reflection of light on a wall or other surface that may be bothersome. • Check to see if dimming lights or turning off down lights is better for the person with ASD. If there is no scope for change, sunglasses or tinted glasses may be worn inside the depending on the severity of the sensitivity. • Wearing a cap indoors can assist an individual who is sensitive to bright lights if they cannot be turned off.
Sound	Individuals with ASD can often be highly sensitive to and distracted by sounds that their peers may not even notice such as a train far away or the high pitch of a researcher's voice. They can also become distressed at the sound of loud unexpected noises. • Reduce environmental noise where possible by choosing carpeted rooms to reduce echoing as well as the scraping of chairs

(continued)

Table 4.1 (continued)

Factor	Recommendation
	on the floor. • Where possible, warn the individual about sudden noises such as when a fire drill siren may be about to ring. • Encourage the individual to let you know when a particular noise is distracting or painful.
Temperature	Individuals with ASD may react differently to temperatures. They may also have tactile sensitivities that may make it uncomfortable to wear particular clothes etc. • As it is not always possible to adjust room temperatures, encourage individuals to have layers of clothes so as to make themselves comfortable throughout a session. • Try and circulate air as much as possible.
Smells	Smells that may not be detected by others may cause discomfort to individuals who are hypersensitive in this area. • Avoid wearing strong perfumes, after shaves and heavily scented deodorants. • Some individuals may be sensitive to food smells from nearby kitchens or canteens. Consider this when choosing venues.
Family and ASD Friendly Environments	Ensure there is waiting room space for families and siblings if you are working with children, and that these are safe and provide toys/books, for siblings to play with. • Easy access to family friendly bathrooms—large enough for parents and prams, with access to change tables is important. • Consider the bathroom environment—paper towels are better than noisy hand dryers. • If you have a long interview/set of tasks to undertake—consider splitting it into two sessions or providing a break time and area for the person to relax (couch, supportive bean bag, floor cushions, quiet zone) without the requirement for social interaction.

Source: AutismCRC (2014), pp. 12–14.

4.8.6 Setting Up the Room Before the Interview or Focus Group Session Occurs

As with every data collection method, there are factors that researchers should consider before they use interviews or focus groups. Before conducting an interview or focus group session with participants on the autism spectrum the researcher may want to:

- consider an appropriate time when the interview or focus group session should occur so that potential participants can avoid peak hour traffic or entering spaces where there are lots of noise that is generated by a crowd (e.g., class change over periods);
- schedule a start and an end time for the interview or focus group session along with rest times;

- spend time preparing for the interview or focus group session. For instance, organising the tables and chairs in the room and/or placing signage around the building so that participants can navigate to the room where the interview or focus group discussion will be conducted;
- distribute in advance the questions that will be asked during the interview or focus group session so that participants will have the opportunity to formulate their answers;
- invite the participants to individually inspect the room where the interview or focus group session will occur so that they can identify any sensory factors that might disrupt the session. Such an orientation session can also help the participants become familiar with the paths required to get to the room as well as other facilities, such as a bathroom;
- print and distribute materials that will be used during the interview or focus group session, such as consent forms and a list of questions to be discussed during the focus group session; and
- provide name tags so that members of the focus group can identify each other (AutismCRC, 2014; NHMRC, 2018).

4.8.7 *Immediately Before Starting the Interview or Focus Group Session*

Just before an interview or focus group session begins a researcher may wish to assist participants on the autism spectrum to participate in the discussion by using the following strategies:

- before starting the interview or focus group session, the researcher may wish to have a conversation about the guidelines and expectations of participation. For example, the researcher could state that no offensive language or bullying will be tolerated. Furthermore, a researcher could explain to participants that they will not be expected to join an ad hoc discussion instead there will be taking turns to express their views and experiences;
- it might be advantageous for a researcher to explain their credentials and their interest in the topic of the autism spectrum. Such a disclosure can help establish rapport between the researcher and the participant in the interview or focus group; and
- if appropriate, a researcher may ask participants to introduce themselves to others in the focus group so that rapport between members of the focus group can be established (AutismCRC, 2014; NHMRC, 2018).

4.8.8   *During the Interview or Focus Group Sessions*

Once the participant has provided their consent the researcher then needs to facilitate a discussion in the interview or focus group. To help facilitate this discussion the researcher may wish to implement the following strategies:

- provide verbal signposts and cues to help participants understand the course of the discussion. For example, at the appropriate time the researcher could state *"We have one more question to discuss before we have a break for refreshments and the bathroom"*;
- before posing a question the researcher may want to explain how they expect participants to answer the question. For example, they may state *"Can you please briefly describe?"* or *"As briefly as possible . . ."*. Such statements can convey to the participants that the researcher is only expects a succinct answer and not a verbose and detailed response; and
- whilst conducting the interview or focus group session the researcher could speak at a pace that enables others to understand their questions. Furthermore, if needed, a researcher could clarify the terms that they state in a question by providing a definition (AutismCRC, 2014; NHMRC, 2018).

4.8.9   *Providing Research Results to Participants*
on the Autism Spectrum

Once a researcher has finished their study, they may be obligated by their research institution to share their study's findings with the former participants (NHMRC, 2018). To help with this feedback process a researcher may want to use the following strategies:

- some people on the autism spectrum might find a verbal debriefing session socially taxing and stressful. To sidestep this process, an information sheet that describes the study's findings might be more appropriate then a verbal description; and
- once the interview or focus group session has finished the researcher may want to send to the participants a text message, email or letter thanking them for their input into the study. The thank you message should give the participants the opportunity to ask questions or provide feedback about the study. The medium used to communicate with participants will depend on their preferred mode of communication (AutismCRC, 2014; NHMRC, 2018).

4.9 Final Comments

The purpose of this SpringerBrief was to present a snapshot of the current state of research about the experiences and insights of autistics and their sexual behaviours, relationships, sexuality, and gender identity. To achieve this objective a general set of keywords and research questions were formulated as it was expected that the literature about this topic would be extremely diverse. In conjunction with a general set of keywords, four prominent academic databases (i.e., SpringerLink, PubMed, SAGE, Taylor and Francis) were searched as they were deemed to collectively contain a large volume of research about this topic. This process resulted in a large number of possible studies being identified. After applying a strict set of eligibility criterion to the potential studies, 23 studies were included in this scoping review. To ensure that any other eligible studies that were missed during the initial search phase were identified and included the first author examined the reference lists of the 23 studies deemed eligible for examination. This additional step resulted in the inclusion of four additional studies. This two-phased approach towards identifying potential articles for this scoping review resulted in the total inclusion of 27 studies.

An examination of the 27 studies revealed five main themes that were shared among the body of literature. These themes, which were reported in Chap. 3, were: sexual orientation, gender identity, relationship status, online dating, and sexual behaviours. It was discovered that most studies about autistics and their sexual orientation and gender expression concluded that relative to the non-autistic population, a higher proportion of the autistic population do not identify as either heterosexual or cisgender. It was also revealed that autistics tended to be single and tended to learn about sexual behaviours from the internet and other non-social sources of information, such as magazines. Finally, it was discovered that autistics engage in the same types of sexual behaviours as non-autistics.

The five themes that were discovered in the body of examined literature highlighted seven gaps in the research, which were: pregnancy and childbirth, autistics being parents, domestic violence, relationship breakup and divorce, sexual education, contraception, and LGBTQIA+ issues (e.g., coming out, gender reassignment surgery, homophobia, transphobia, etc.). To ensure that these were actually gaps an additional search of the autism literature about these topics were conducted using the same four databases that were used during the initial search procedures. For example, the terms *'coming out'* and *'autis*'* was searched on SpringerLink and then the same search process was repeated on PubMed, Sage, and Taylor and Francis. By conducting these additional searches these gaps in the literature were able to be confirmed. Additionally, these extra searches ensured that the methodological approach used in this scoping review to retrieve studies for the original analysis was comprehensive.

Perhaps the most striking finding from this scoping review was the contrasts within the literature between the large number of studies in which autistics explain their sexual behaviours and insights and the lack of literature about how best to support them as sexual beings. For example, multiple studies have shown that autistics have a greater likelihood of identifying as being homosexual yet there is a lack of literature about their experiences of homophobia and coming out. Similarly, the literature indicates that autistics are less inclined to identify as being cisgender, yet no literature was found about their experiences of transphobia or gender reassignment surgery. The lack of qualitative information about such topics has already been raised by researchers. Bennett and Goodall (2016), for example, have claimed that by not exploring the homophobic experiences of non-heterosexual autistics policies and strategies specifically designed to help them have not been produced. In the interests of improving the health and wellbeing of autistics who are sexually active it is important that the insights from autistics about the seven identified gaps which this scoping review discovered be researched.

In summary, a diverse range of studies about autistics and their experiences and views about sexual behaviours, relationships, sexuality, and gender identity were examined. The collection of such studies was only possible due to a broad research focus, entering a list of general key words into four prominent electronic academic repositories, and then using a clear set of eligibility criteria to determine which studies should be either included or excluded from the analysis phase of the scoping review. This academic exercise helped the objective of the scoping review be achieved, namely to present a snapshot of the current state of research about the experiences and insights of autistics about their sexual behaviours, relationships, sexuality, and gender identity.

References

Ainsworth, T. A., & Spiegel, J. H. (2010). Quality of life of individuals with and without facial feminization surgery or gender reassignment surgery. *Quality of Life Research, 19*(7), 1019–1024. https://doi.org/10.1007/s11136-010-9668-7

American Psychiatric Association (APA). (2013). *Diagnostic and statistical manual of mental disorders (DSM-5®)*. American Psychiatric Pub.

Ballan, M. S., & Freyer, M. B. (2012). Self-defense among women with disabilities: An unexplored domain in domestic violence cases. *Violence Against Women, 18*(9), 1083–1107. https://doi.org/10.1177/1077801212461430

Barnett, J. P. (2017). Intersectional harassment and deviant embodiment among Autistic adults:(dis) ability, gender and sexuality. *Culture, Health & Sexuality, 19*(11), 1210–1224. https://doi.org/10.1080/13691058.2017.1309070

Barnett, J. P., & Maticka-Tyndale, E. (2015). Qualitative exploration of sexual experiences among adults on the autism spectrum: Implications for sex education. *Perspectives on Sexual and Reproductive Health, 47*(4), 171–179. https://doi.org/10.1363/47e5715

Bennett, M., & Goodall, E. (2016). Towards an agenda for research for lesbian, gay, bisexual, transgendered and/or intersexed people with an Autism Spectrum Diagnosis. *Journal of Autism and Developmental Disorders, 46*(9), 3190–3192. https://doi.org/10.1007/s10803-016-2844-z

Bennett, M., Webster, A. A., Goodall, E., & Rowland, S. (2018). Intimacy and romance across the autism spectrum: Unpacking the "not interested in sex" myth. In *Life on the autism spectrum* (pp. 195–211). Singapore: Springer. https://doi.org/10.1007/978-981-13-3359-0_10

Bonis, S. (2016). Stress and parents of children with autism: A review of literature. *Issues in Mental Health Nursing, 37*(3), 153–163. https://doi.org/10.3109/01612840.2015.1116030

Brennan, J. (2018). Gay men and the coming out of Colton Haynes. *Celebrity Studies, 9*(1), 109–113. https://doi.org/10.1080/19392397.2017.1346053

Bush, H. H. (2019). Dimensions of sexuality among young women, with and without autism, with predominantly sexual minority identities. *Sexuality and Disability, 37*(2), 275–292. https://doi.org/10.1007/s11195-018-9532-1

Cascio, M. A., Weiss, J. A., Racine, E., & Autism Research Ethics Task Force. (2020). Person-oriented ethics for autism research: Creating best practices through engagement with autism and autistic communities. *Autism,* 1362361320918763. https://doi.org/10.1177/1362361320918763

Cheuk, S., & Lashewicz, B. (2016). How are they doing? Listening as fathers of children with autism spectrum disorder compare themselves to fathers of children who are typically developing. *Autism, 20*(3), 343–352. https://doi.org/10.1177/1362361315584464

Cleland, J., Magrath, R., & Kian, E. (2018). The internet as a site of decreasing cultural homophobia in association football: An online response by fans to the coming out of Thomas Hitzlsperger. *Men and Masculinities, 21*(1), 91–111. https://doi.org/10.1177/1097184X16663261

Clements-Nolle, K., Marx, R., & Katz, M. (2006). Attempted suicide among transgender persons: The influence of gender-based discrimination and victimization. *Journal of Homosexuality, 51* (3), 53–69. https://doi.org/10.1300/J082v51n03_04

Cooperative Research Centre for Living with Autism Spectrum Disorders (AutismCRC). (2014). *Inclusive Research Practice Guides and Checklists for Autism Spectrum Research.* Australia: The University of Queensland.

Cooper, K., Smith, L. G., & Russell, A. J. (2018). Gender identity in autism: Sex differences in social affiliation with gender groups. *Journal of Autism and Developmental Disorders, 48*(12), 3995–4006. https://doi.org/10.1007/s10803-018-3590-1

Corona, L. L., Fox, S. A., Christodulu, K. V., & Worlock, J. A. (2016). Providing education on sexuality and relationships to adolescents with autism spectrum disorder and their parents. *Sexuality and Disability, 34*(2), 199–214. https://doi.org/10.1007/s11195-015-9424-6

Couch, K. A., Tamborini, C. R., & Reznik, G. L. (2015). The long-term health implications of marital disruption: Divorce, work limits, and social security disability benefits among men. *Demography, 52*(5), 1487–1512. https://doi.org/10.1007/s13524-015-0424-z

Craig, S. L., & McInroy, L. (2014). You can form a part of yourself online: The influence of new media on identity development and coming out for LGBTQ youth. *Journal of Gay & Lesbian Mental Health, 18*(1), 95–109. https://doi.org/10.1080/19359705.2013.777007

De Vaus, D., Gray, M., Qu, L., & Stanton, D. (2017). The economic consequences of divorce in six OECD countries. *Australian Journal of Social Issues, 52*(2), 180–199. https://doi.org/10.1002/ajs4.13

Dean, M., Harwood, R., & Kasari, C. (2017). The art of camouflage: Gender differences in the social behaviors of girls and boys with autism spectrum disorder. *Autism, 21*(6), 678–689. https://doi.org/10.1177/1362361316671845

Dekker, L. P., van der Vegt, E. J., Visser, K., Tick, N., Boudesteijn, F., Verhulst, F. C., et al. (2015). Improving psychosexual knowledge in adolescents with autism spectrum disorder: Pilot of the tackling teenage training program. *Journal of Autism and Developmental Disorders, 45*(6), 1532–1540. https://doi.org/10.1007/s10803-014-2301-9

Dentato, M. P., Craig, S. L., Lloyd, M. R., Kelly, B. L., Wright, C., & Austin, A. (2016). Homophobia within schools of social work: The critical need for affirming classroom settings and effective preparation for service with the LGBTQ community. *Social Work Education, 35* (6), 672–692. https://doi.org/10.1080/02615479.2016.1150452

Dewinter, J., De Graaf, H., & Begeer, S. (2017). Sexual orientation, gender identity, and romantic relationships in adolescents and adults with autism spectrum disorder. *Journal of Autism and Developmental Disorders, 47*(9), 2927–2934. https://doi.org/10.1007/s10803-017-3199-9

Fielden, S. L., & Jepson, H. (2016). An exploration into the career experiences of lesbians in the UK. *Gender in Management: An International Journal, 31*(4), 281–296. https://doi.org/10.1108/GM-03-2016-0037

Fisher, H., & Low, H. (2015). Financial implications of relationship breakdown: Does marriage matter? *Review of Economics of the Household, 13*(4), 735–769. https://doi.org/10.1007/s11150-015-9292-y

Fletcher-Watson, S., Adams, J., Brook, K., Charman, T., Crane, L., Cusack, J., et al. (2019). Making the future together: Shaping autism research through meaningful participation. *Autism, 23*(4), 943–953. https://doi.org/10.1177/1362361318786721

Gardner, M., Suplee, P. D., Bloch, J., & Lecks, K. (2016). Exploratory study of childbearing experiences of women with Asperger syndrome. *Nursing for Women's Health, 20*(1), 28–37. https://doi.org/10.1016/j.nwh.2015.12.001

George, R., & Stokes, M. A. (2018). A quantitative analysis of mental health among sexual and gender minority groups in ASD. *Journal of Autism and Developmental Disorders, 48*(6), 2052–2063. https://doi.org/10.1007/s10803-018-3469-1

Goodall, E. (2016). *The autism spectrum guide to sexuality and relationships: Understand yourself and make choices that are right for you.* Jessica Kingsley Publishers.

Gould, J. (2017). Towards understanding the under-recognition of girls and women on the autism spectrum. *Autism, 21*(6), 703–705. https://doi.org/10.1177/1362361317706174

Griffiths, S., Allison, C., Kenny, R., Holt, R., Smith, P., & Baron-Cohen, S. (2019). The Vulnerability Experiences Quotient (VEQ): A study of vulnerability, mental health and life satisfaction in autistic adults. *Autism Research, 12*(10), 1516–1528. https://doi.org/10.1002/aur.2162

Hollocks, M. J., Lerh, J. W., Magiati, I., Meiser-Stedman, R., & Brugha, T. S. (2019). Anxiety and depression in adults with autism spectrum disorder: A systematic review and meta-analysis. *Psychological Medicine, 49*(4), 559–572. https://doi.org/10.1017/S0033291718002283

Holmes, L. G., & Himle, M. B. (2014). Brief report: Parent–child sexuality communication and autism spectrum disorders. *Journal of Autism and Developmental Disorders, 44*(11), 2964–2970. https://doi.org/10.1007/s10803-014-2146-2

Holmes, L. G., Strassberg, D. S., & Himle, M. B. (2019). Family sexuality communication for adolescent girls on the autism spectrum. *Journal of Autism and Developmental Disorders, 49*(6), 2403–2416. https://doi.org/10.1007/s10803-019-03904-6

Howell, G. (2018). Sexual orientation and gender diversity in the workplace. In *Diversity and inclusion in the global workplace* (pp. 69–79). Cham: Palgrave Macmillan. https://doi.org/10.1007/978-3-319-54993-4_4

Humphrey, N., & Hebron, J. (2015). Bullying of children and adolescents with autism spectrum conditions: A state of the field review. *International Journal of Inclusive Education, 19*(8), 845–862. https://doi.org/10.1080/13603116.2014.981602

Hunt, Q. A., Morrow, Q. J., & McGuire, J. K. (2019). Experiences of suicide in transgender youth: A qualitative, community-based study. *Archives of Suicide Research*, 1–16. https://doi.org/10.1080/13811118.2019.1610677

Jang, J., Matson, J. L., Adams, H. L., Konst, M. J., Cervantes, P. E., & Goldin, R. L. (2014). What are the ages of persons studied in autism research: A 20-year review. *Research in Autism Spectrum Disorders, 8*(12), 1756–1760. https://doi.org/10.1016/j.rasd.2014.08.008

Jensen, A. A. (2018). Gender and the transsexual body in Transamerica. *Literator (Potchefstroom. Online), 39*(1), 1–6.

Kuiper, M. W., Verhoeven, E. W., & Geurts, H. M. (2019). Stop making noise! Auditory sensitivity in adults with an autism spectrum disorder diagnosis: Physiological habituation and subjective detection thresholds. *Journal of Autism and Developmental Disorders, 49*(5), 2116–2128. https://doi.org/10.1007/s10803-019-03890-9

Livingston, L. A., Colvert, E., Social Relationships Study Team, Bolton, P., & Happé, F. (2019). Good social skills despite poor theory of mind: Exploring compensation in autism spectrum disorder. *Journal of Child Psychology and Psychiatry, 60*(1), 102–110. https://doi.org/10.1111/jcpp.12886

Lovelock, M. (2017). 'Is every YouTuber going to make a coming out video eventually?': YouTube celebrity video bloggers and lesbian and gay identity. *Celebrity Studies, 8*(1), 87–103. https://doi.org/10.1080/19392397.2016.1214608

Mackin, M. L., Loew, N., Gonzalez, A., Tykol, H., & Christensen, T. (2016). Parent perceptions of sexual education needs for their children with autism. *Journal of Pediatric Nursing, 31*(6), 608–618. https://doi.org/10.1016/j.pedn.2016.07.003

Marks, L. (2020, March 12). *Why adults with autism need sex education.* Spectrum I Autism Research News. https://www.spectrumnews.org/opinion/viewpoint/why-adults-with-autism-need-sex-education/

Maschi, T., Rees, J., & Klein, E. (2016). "Coming Out" of prison: An exploratory study of LGBT elders in the criminal justice system. *Journal of Homosexuality, 63*(9), 1277–1295. https://doi.org/10.1080/00918369.2016.1194093

May, T., Pang, K. C., & Williams, K. (2017). Brief report: Sexual attraction and relationships in adolescents with autism. *Journal of Autism and Developmental Disorders, 47*(6), 1910–1916. https://doi.org/10.1007/s10803-017-3092-6

McKeever, M., & Wolfinger, N. H. (2001). Reexamining the economic costs of marital disruption for women. *Social Science Quarterly, 82*(1), 202–217. https://doi.org/10.1111/0038-4941.00018

Meadan, H., Stoner, J. B., & Angell, M. E. (2015). Fathers of children with autism: Perceived roles, responsibilities, and support needs. *Early Child Development and Care, 185*(10), 1678–1694. https://doi.org/10.1080/03004430.2015.1019876

Mizock, L., Woodrum, T. D., Riley, J., Sotilleo, E. A., Yuen, N., & Ormerod, A. J. (2017). Coping with transphobia in employment: Strategies used by transgender and gender-diverse people in the United States. *International Journal of Transgenderism, 18*(3), 282–294. https://doi.org/10.1080/15532739.2017.1304313

Mogavero, M. C., & Hsu, K. H. (2019). Dating and courtship behaviors among those with autism spectrum disorder. *Sexuality and Disability*, 1–10. https://doi.org/10.1007/s11195-019-09565-8

Muratori, F., Tonacci, A., Billeci, L., Catalucci, T., Igliozzi, R., Calderoni, S., et al. (2017). Olfactory processing in male children with autism: Atypical odor threshold and identification. *Journal of Autism and Developmental Disorders, 47*(10), 3243–3251. https://doi.org/10.1007/s10803-017-3250-x

National Health and Medical Research Council (NHMRC). (2018). *National Statement on Ethical Conduct in Human Research: 2007 (Updated 2018).* Retrieved from https://www.nhmrc.gov.au/about-us/publications/national-statement-ethical-conduct-human-research-2007-updated-2018

Nichols, S., & Blakeley-Smith, A. (2009). "I'm not sure we're ready for this...": Working with families toward facilitating healthy sexuality for individuals with autism spectrum disorders. *Social Work in Mental Health, 8*(1), 72–91. https://doi.org/10.1080/15332980902932383

O'Halloran, M., Sweeney, J., & Doody, O. (2013). Exploring fathers' perceptions of parenting a child with Asperger syndrome. *Journal of Intellectual Disabilities, 17*(3), 198–213. https://doi.org/10.1177/1744629513494928

Organization for autism research (OAR). (2019). *Sex Ed for Self-Advocates.* Sex Ed for Self-Advocates. https://researchautism.org/sex-ed-guide/

Pryde, R., & Jahoda, A. (2018). A qualitative study of mothers' experiences of supporting the sexual development of their sons with autism and an accompanying intellectual disability. *International Journal of Developmental Disabilities, 64*(3), 166–174. https://doi.org/10.1080/20473869.2018.1446704

Rankin, J. A., Paisley, C. A., Tomeny, T. S., & Eldred, S. W. (2019). Fathers of youth with autism spectrum disorder: A systematic review of the impact of fathers' involvement on youth, families, and intervention. *Clinical Child and Family Psychology Review, 22*(4), 458–477. https://doi.org/10.1007/s10567-019-00294-0

Rogers, C., Lepherd, L., Ganguly, R., & Jacob-Rogers, S. (2017). Perinatal issues for women with high functioning autism spectrum disorder. *Women and Birth, 30*(2), e89–e95. https://doi.org/10.1016/j.wombi.2016.09.009

Roth, M. E., & Gillis, J. M. (2015). Convenience with the click of a mouse: A survey of adults with autism spectrum disorder on online dating. *Sexuality and Disability, 33*(1), 133–150. https://doi.org/10.1007/s11195-014-9392-2

Roth, M. Y., Page, S. T., & Bremner, W. J. (2016). Male hormonal contraception: Looking back and moving forward. *Andrology, 4*(1), 4–12. https://doi.org/10.1111/andr.12110

Schuwerk, T., Vuori, M., & Sodian, B. (2015). Implicit and explicit theory of mind reasoning in autism spectrum disorders: The impact of experience. *Autism, 19*(4), 459–468. https://doi.org/10.1177/1362361314526004

Sears, J. T., & Williams, W. L. (1997). *Overcoming heterosexism and homophobia: Strategies that work*. New York, NY: Columbia University Press.

Selvaggi, G., & Bellringer, J. (2011). Gender reassignment surgery: An overview. *Nature Reviews Urology, 8*(5), 274–282. https://doi.org/10.1038/nrurol.2011.46

Sim, A., Cordier, R., Vaz, S., & Falkmer, T. (2019). "We are in this together": Experiences of relationship satisfaction in couples raising a child with autism spectrum disorder. *Research in Autism Spectrum Disorders, 58*, 39–51. https://doi.org/10.1016/j.rasd.2018.11.011

Skew, A., Evans, A., & Gray, E. (2009). Repartnering in the United Kingdom and Australia. *Journal of Comparative Family Studies, 40*(4), 563–585. https://doi.org/10.3138/jcfs.40.4.563

Strang, J. F., Powers, M. D., Knauss, M., Sibarium, E., Leibowitz, S. F., Kenworthy, L., et al. (2018). "They thought it was an obsession": Trajectories and perspectives of autistic transgender and gender-diverse adolescents. *Journal of Autism and Developmental Disorders, 48*(12), 4039–4055. https://doi.org/10.1007/s10803-018-3723-6

Strang, J. F., van der Miesen, A. I., Caplan, R., Hughes, C., daVanport, S., & Lai, M. C. (2020). Both sex-and gender-related factors should be considered in autism research and clinical practice. *Autism*. https://doi.org/10.1177/1362361320913192

Strifert, K. (2014). The link between oral contraceptive use and prevalence in autism spectrum disorder. *Medical Hypotheses, 83*(6), 718–725. https://doi.org/10.1016/j.mehy.2014.09.026

Tach, L. M., & Eads, A. (2015). Trends in the economic consequences of marital and cohabitation dissolution in the United States. *Demography, 52*(2), 401–432. https://doi.org/10.1007/s13524-015-0374-5

Tamborini, C. R., Couch, K. A., & Reznik, G. L. (2015). Long-term impact of divorce on women's earnings across multiple divorce windows: A life course perspective. *Advances in Life Course Research, 26*, 44–59. https://doi.org/10.1016/j.alcr.2015.06.001

Tullis, C. A., & Zangrillo, A. N. (2013). Sexuality education for adolescents and adults with autism spectrum disorders. *Psychology in the Schools, 50*(9), 866–875. https://doi.org/10.1002/pits.21713

Visser, K., Greaves-Lord, K., Tick, N. T., Verhulst, F. C., Maras, A., & van der Vegt, E. J. (2015). Study protocol: A randomized controlled trial investigating the effects of a psychosexual training program for adolescents with autism spectrum disorder. *BMC Psychiatry, 15*(1), 207. https://doi.org/10.1186/s12888-015-0586-7

Wakefield, J. R., Kalinauskaite, M., & Hopkins, N. (2016). The nation and the family: The impact of national identification and perceived importance of family values on homophobic attitudes in Lithuania and Scotland. *Sex Roles, 75*(9–10), 448–458. https://doi.org/10.1007/s11199-016-0641-y

Wang, C., Festin, M. P., & Swerdloff, R. S. (2016). Male hormonal contraception: Where are we now? *Current Obstetrics and Gynecology Reports, 5*(1), 38–47. https://doi.org/10.1007/s13669-016-0140-8

Wicker, B., Monfardini, E., & Royet, J. P. (2016). Olfactory processing in adults with autism spectrum disorders. *Molecular Autism, 7*(1), 1–11. https://doi.org/10.1186/s13229-016-0070-3

Wilson, A. D. (2018). "Put it in your shoe it will make you limp": British men's online responses to a male pill. *The Journal of Men's Studies, 26*(3), 247–265. https://doi.org/10.1177/1060826518761433

Wuest, B. (2014). Stories like mine: Coming out videos and queer identities on YouTube. In *Queer youth and media cultures* (pp. 19–33). London: Palgrave Macmillan. https://doi.org/10.1057/9781137383556_2